# Explosive Power and Jumping Ability for All Sports:
## Atlas of Exercises

D0937564

# Explosive Power and Jumping Ability for All Sports: Atlas of Exercises

## Tadeusz Starzynski and Henryk Sozanski, Ph.D.

### Translated by Thomas Kurz

**STADION**®
www.stadion.com

# Explosive Power and Jumping Ability for All Sports: Atlas of Exercises

**by Tadeusz Starzynski and Henryk Sozanski, Ph.D.**

Published by:

Stadion Publishing Company, Inc.
Post Office Box 447
Island Pond, VT 05846, U.S.A.
www.stadion.com

Originally published as *Trening Skocznosci: Atlas Cwiczen*
Copyright © 1995 by Resortowe Centrum Metodyczno-Szkoleniowe Kultury Fizycznej i Sportu
Polish language revision copyright © 1999 by Tadeusz Starzynski and Henryk Sozanski
Translation copyright © 1999 by Thomas Kurz

All rights reserved. No part of this book may be reproduced in any form or by any means without written permission from the publisher, except for brief quotations included in a review.

**Publisher's Cataloging in Publication**
*(Provided by Quality Books, Inc.)*

Starzynski, Tadeusz.
    Explosive power and jumping ability for all
  sports : atlas of exercises / Tadeusz Starzynski
  and Henryk Sozanski. — 1st ed.
    p. cm.
    Includes bibliographical references and index.
    LCCN: 99-70772
    ISBN: 0-940149-09-5


    1. Jumping—Training. 2. Physical education and training.
  3. Exercise.  I. Sozanski, Henryk. II. Title.

GV1073.S83 1999                    796.43'2
                          QBI99-106

Translation: Thomas Kurz
Editing: R. Scott Perry
Illustrations: Piotr Szczepaniak
Cover Design: Tamara Dever, TLC Graphics
Book Design: Mikolaj Zagorski
Printed in the United States of America

# Preface

It is difficult to find a sports discipline that does not call on various forms of jumping ability or explosive strength. While theoreticians still search for explosive power's place in the model of motor abilities, coaches every day must solve practical methodological tasks that have to do with developing jumping ability or explosive strength specific to a particular discipline of sports or event.

Literature on this subject is scarce. Explosive strength is placed between strength and speed. Theoreticians have counted on the hope that some peculiar combination of training in these two fundamental abilities will give the sought-after capability— namely, explosive strength. At the same time practitioners—coaches—have worked out several original training solutions, effectively developing specific forms of explosive strength or jumping ability. Explosive strength as jumping ability manifests itself in the fullest in track-and-field jumps, so the significant international successes of Polish athletes in these events are good proof of an effective technology of explosive strength training. These records attest to it: World records, in long jump of Elzbieta Krzesinska (women, 635 cm in 1956), triple jump of Józef Szmidt (17.03 m in 1960) and Zdzislaw Hoffman (17.42 m in 1983), pole vault of Wladyslaw Kozakiewicz (578 cm in 1980), high jump of Jacek Wszola (235 cm in 1980); gold medals of Elzbieta Krzesinska (long jump, 1956), Józef Szmidt (triple jump, 1964), Tadeusz Slusarski (pole vault, 1976), Wladyslaw Kozakiewicz (pole vault, 1980).

It is worthwhile to gather these experiences as a step toward organizing and systematizing knowledge on training for explosive strength. The worked out examples will help coaches of other sports because the principles of training are universal, differing only in goals and the ways explosive strength shows itself in different sports. We believe this work will be particularly useful for coaches, instructors, teachers, and athletes at all levels of experience.

# Warning-Disclaimer

Stadion Publishing Company, Inc. and this book's creators, authors, advisors, consultants, editors, printers, wholesalers, distributors, and retailers are not liable or responsible, in whole or in part, to any person or entity for any injury, damage, or loss of any sort caused or alleged to be caused directly or indirectly by the use, practice, teaching, or other dissemination of any of the techniques, information, or ideas presented in this book. The information in this book is presented for educational purposes only.

Consult your physician before starting any exercise program.

# Table of Contents

# Jumping Ability in an Athlete's Preparation

# Definition of Terms and Classifications of Sports

*Note from translator about the use of terms:*

*The terms* explosive strength *and* explosive power *mean the same. Explosive strength is the ability to rapidly increase force (Tidow 1990). The steeper the increase of strength in time the greater the explosive strength.*

Jumping ability is a manifestation of explosive strength in the form of a jump. Examples of other manifestations of explosive strength are punches or the arm action in shot put. Whenever the authors describe principles of training for jumping ability, what they say will also apply to any explosive strength training.

*The term* speed-strength[*] *refers to forms of strength used in fast movements and to amortize, or damp the force of, fast-moving objects as, for example, catching a hard-thrown object or executing a landing. These are not forms of pure speed because of the large amount of muscular tension involved in speed-strength movements. Development of explosive strength, or jumping ability, is one of the objectives of speed-strength training.*

Jumps play an important role in many sports disciplines. During the phase of flight, lack of ground contact means an athlete cannot change the trajectory of movement, but often has to perform complex tasks related to the sports contest (e.g., basketball throw, catch, volleyball block, jumping kick). Doing these tasks well depends on one's level of jumping ability (Mroczynski and Starzynski 1994).

What is this ability? How can it be defined? What elements does it depend on? Where does it belong in an understanding of an athlete's preparation?

In the *Small Encyclopedia of Sports (Mala Encyclopedia Sportu)*, jumping ability is defined.

*Jumping ability ... is a many-faceted movement ability depending on, among other factors: body build and proportions of the athlete, speed, strength, and elasticity of the muscles taking part in the takeoff as well as on neuromuscular coordination. Jumping ability is developed mainly through the repetitive method, aiming foremost to increase the explosive strength of the muscles taking part in the takeoff, mastering the skill of performing very fast movements in a form similar to the jump, mobilizing for those movements the highest possible muscle power output, and—in events calling for jumping high repeatedly—developing sport-specific jumping endurance. Jumping ability can be fairly precisely measured, for example, by a reach jump* (Hadzelek 1986).

---

[*] This term—*speed-strength* as used in this book—is not to be confused with the term "speed strength" (no hyphen) used by other authors to denote the result of dividing one's maximal strength value in a given movement by the time it takes to reach that value.

As is evident, jumping ability is a complex ability depending on many factors. Being a natural component of an athlete's preparation, jumping ability ought to be developed purposely for specific tasks—those typical for a given sport discipline. This is the way to raise an athlete's performance.

Particular sports have different functional needs in relation to jumping ability. From this point of view we can classify them in the following groups.

- Sports and events in which jumping ability is the leading ability in the athlete's fitness preparation—for example, track-and-field jumps, or jumps in gymnastics and acrobatics

- Sports and events in which jumping ability is of equal importance with some other ability or abilities, and jumping tasks are a constant element of the sport's movement skills—for example, the majority of ball games, gymnastics, acrobatics, and springboard and platform diving

- Sports and events in which jumping occurs in solving some situations depending on the circumstances—for example, lawn tennis, table tennis, badminton, and downhill skiing

- Sports and events in which the power of legs and hips plays an essential role in the athlete's fitness preparation; this property (powerful legs and hips) does not manifest itself as jumping ability during the contest, but the training for these sports develops it—for example, weightlifting, track-and-field throws, and ski jumps

This is the simplest classification. It is possible, of course, to delve deeper into the demands of particular sports and the needs of particular athletes. Here we wanted only to draw attention to the issue, to show how widespread are the applications for developing jumping ability. Because of the interrelations among movement abilities, neither the coach nor the athlete can consider jumping ability separately from other abilities. Its place in an athlete's preparation depends on a given sport and on the athlete's age and experience.

# Physical Fitness Training

## What Is Fitness Preparation?

Physical fitness is movement potential that determines an athlete's readiness for solving movement tasks. Physical fitness depends on an athlete's level of speed, strength, movement coordination, and endurance as fundamental movement abilities, along with other abilities and properties that permit the person to function effectively (Balsevich and Zaporozhnov 1987).

Fitness depends on many factors. What qualifies as fitness changes with an athlete's age, and it forms under the influence of sports training. The starting point is developing general, versatile fitness, building up one's natural movement potential. Then, gradually the athlete enters the stage of developing called directed fitness that prepares him or her for sport-specific fitness. The athlete starts with developing general movement fitness, then proceeds to exercises more like the efforts of a particular sport, and finally to sport-specific training according to the sport's needs and his or her needs. The road toward high results always begins with versatile development of fitness. We take that into consideration already when guiding planning, marking three sequential stages of the development of fitness: general, directed, and finally, sport-specific.

The above division of fitness development into stages naturally affects what exercises the athlete or coach selects for training. The whole collection of exercises in this work can be divided into three basic groups: versatile or general exercises, directed exercises, and sport-specific exercises (Sozanski and Sledziewski 1989). What are the principles of this division?

**General exercises** are those that are nonspecific for a given sport and that harmoniously develop all systems of the body. The purpose of these exercises is to prepare an individual for future specialization. We include in this category all track and field events, games and plays, ball games, gymnastics and acrobatics, winter sports, swimming, and other forms of overall activity. At the initial stage of fitness development, those exercises should be used widely.

**Directed exercises** are those that in their external or internal structure are in some way similar to the whole or a part of competitive task (sports technique). For a track-and-field jumper, for example, those exercises will concern themselves with jumping, speed and strength of the legs and trunk, flexibility, coordination, and agility. Forms of training at the directed stage of fitness development are still very varied, from games and playing up to a strict form of particular sports events.

**Sport-specific exercises** are those immediately developing sport-specific fitness for a given event. These exercises preserve both the internal and external structure of movement of the competitive exercise. Simply put, they must be as close as possible to the particular phases of movements that occur in an athlete's competitive technique.

Each of these exercise groups corresponds roughly with subsequent stages of training, so that general exercises predominate at the stage of versatile (general) fitness preparation and the most use of sport-specific exercises is made at the stage of sport-specific fitness preparation. At every stage, season, and training cycle, however, the athlete can use exercises from more than one group, often even in a single workout. Here is an example: A beginning track-and-field athlete prepares for a composite event that includes a long jump, so the athlete uses, even though to a small extent, sport-specific exercises. An advanced athlete, commencing training after a transition period between seasons, does not start work with sport-specific exercises but gradually takes them up, beginning first with general exercises and then moving to directed exercises. A good example of a sensible chain of exercises is a warm-up in which the athlete proceeds from general exercises (jog, lean in any direction, arm swings, leg raises), through directed (hops, jumps), to sport-specific (technical elements of jumps practiced on the grass), and finally the actual technique (long jump from the runway).

In many disciplines of sports speed-strength fitness is of decisive importance in conjunction with movement coordination. We want the athlete to bounce like a ball, i.e., have the greatest possible jumping ability, while at the same time being able to exquisitely steer his or her body and perform complex technical tasks characteristic of the sport. These goals must be reflected in the model of fitness preparation, which is the challenge to the authors.

*We begin with multi-event preparation at the first stage of long-term training, so right from the start of the directed stage of training, this athlete-ball is able to work on achieving the greatest possible dynamism of takeoff and the most effective self-steering in particular phases of the competitive technique.*

Through appropriate training the athlete achieves a high level of speed-strength fitness, permitting performance of dynamic movements with high acceleration, large amplitude, and that are well-directed in space. We introduce the principles of such training while breaking it into separate abilities (speed, strength, explosive strength or jumping ability, coordination) because each of them has its own dynamic of training. The effect of training to develop these seemingly separate abilities, however, must be cohesive—must form one sport-specific model of fitness. Particular elements of preparation cannot manifest themselves independently of each other but must form one functional whole—not strength for strength's sake or flexibility for flexibility's sake, but everything to suit requirements of the given sports discipline.

The athlete must spread the process of developing sports fitness over several years, dividing long-term training into stages. Although speed, strength, and coordination are leading abilities for many sports, they cannot be developed separately from other abilities. This is why the athlete and the coach must consider fundamentals and the important principles of training for all abilities. Every ability brings a definite contribution to the model of sports fitness (Grosser, Starischka, and Zimmerman 1989; Vierkhoshanskiy 1988).

With regard to an athlete's fitness preparation, all the training issues divide themselves into three groups.

1. Speed-strength preparation

2. Developing the ability to steer one's movements

3. Endurance preparation, which is to be understood as fundamental to all other training activities

The preceding three-part division both highlights fundamental areas of training and reveals the training process as a complex entity rather than as a sum of separate actions.

## Speed-strength Preparation

### Training for Speed

For many sports disciplines speed is a very important ability. Speed is the ability to perform movements in the shortest time periods. The level of speed is determined by three of its components: reaction time, velocity of a single movement, and frequency of movements.

Velocity of a movement depends above all on the magnitude of overcome resistance. For athletes of most disciplines this resistance is the mass of their own body. For developing maximal velocity of a simple movement, particular muscle groups must work together in superb fashion, which depends on the efficiency of the nervous system and proper neuromuscular coordination.

The maximal velocity that can be displayed in a given movement depends also on other factors—level of strength, coordination, flexibility, and technical skill. In practice the athlete training for speed deals most often with a complex manifestation of the parameters of speed. Movements performed at maximal velocities have two phases: 1) of increasing velocity, or gathering momentum, which is characterized by achievement of maximal starting acceleration; and 2) of relative stabilization of velocity, i.e., of maintaining the highest velocity while performing the remainder of a given movement.

The structure of any particular technique, in any sports discipline, consists of a definite sequence of phases of movement. The progression of each phase significantly affects the next phase (for example, the velocity of one's prerun affects the velocity of takeoff). Besides practicing the whole technique, it is reasonable also to develop speed analytically, practicing particular phases of technique. Such conduct should always be subordinated to the principal goal of speed training—developing maximal sport-specific speed in accord with the demands of the sports discipline.

The most commonly applied way of developing speed is repeating movements with maximal velocity. Training of this kind must meet three fundamental conditions:

1. The technique of the exercise must permit performing the movement with extreme velocity.

2. Exercises must be mastered so well that an athlete can focus attention solely on the velocity of movement, and not its form.

3. The time of an exercise or the number of repetitions (for example, takeoffs) per set has to be established such that velocity does not diminish before the end of a set because of fatigue.

The chief goal of speed training is for the athlete to exceed his or her maximal velocity in a given movement, a goal reached by the interaction of the duration of each exercise, number of repetitions, and time and character of rest breaks (i.e., passive rest or active rest and what activity during that active rest). The duration of exercise or the distance to be covered is set so that the intensity of work (for example, the velocity of running) can be constant throughout and the athlete in each repetition can be striving for the highest velocity. Select the number of repetitions so the athlete can still do the last repetition in a set at the maximal velocity.

In this repetitive method for speed training, an essential role is played by rest breaks, which ought to ensure optimal recovery. They should not be too long. The athlete should begin the next set of repetitions while still in a state of activation. On the other hand, the receding of fatigue takes time, so the duration of a rest break will vary between 5-12 minutes, depending on the athlete's experience and the difficulty of the exercise. Rest breaks in speed training are always too brief for full recovery because by the time an athlete recovers fully his or her activation level is too low to repeat the exercise with maximal velocity. Fatigue asserts itself relatively quickly, therefore, manifesting itself as a lowering of velocity. Lowering of the velocity of movements is a sign to stop the exercise because further repetitions would not develop speed.

Speed in a pure form practically does not occur. Its external manifestation—speed of performing a movement—is always dependent not only on the components of speed (reaction time, velocity of a single movement, and frequency of movements) but also on other abilities (strength, coordination, endurance, for example). Nevertheless the task of developing speed cannot be equated with developing all these other abilities. Even though in large part the training tasks of developing speed and these other abilities are solved jointly, speed training has its own specific requirements. To increase the speed of competitive techniques, work on those movement abilities that directly influence extreme speed of movement. This is what specificity of tasks for developing speed within fitness preparation is all about.

The main means of developing speed are exercises performed at extreme or near extreme intensity. For this type of work, short duration exercises of 5-15 seconds and relatively low or no external resistance are typical.

Various sprints, jumping ability exercises, and games that stress speed are used as general speed exercises. At the initial stage of long-term training, as well as at the beginning of preparatory period of each yearly or semiannual training cycle, such general speed exercises are an effective means of general, versatile speed development. One must not expect a direct transfer of this general speed to a sport-specific speed in one's sports discipline, however. That transfer will be accomplished through the use of directed and sport-specific speed exercises.

In selecting sport-specific speed exercises, the athlete or coach must pay especially careful attention to the structural similarity of the exercises to the sports technique. In the majority of cases, these exercises consist of part or the whole form of a technique, often altered in such a way as to make it possible to do it at a speed higher than the typical competitive speed. Applying sport-specific exercises to stimulate development of speed, with resistance, this resistance ought to be less than when developing strength and typical speed-strength abilities. Because in most sports competitive actions are done without external resistance, the sport-specific exercises with resistance (often used) will not fully match the sport-specific requirements of just the right mix of speed and strength. In this case we would like to stress the importance of the appropriate choice of sport-specific speed-strength exercises not only with external resistance but also without it. Jumps are a good example of the latter.

Sport-specific exercises are the methodology foundation for developing speed of movements. They are used in repetitive methods as well as methods varying speed and acceleration according to an assigned program.

The development of speed demands a particularly careful balancing of these two methods—repetitive and varying—in a long-term training plan as well as in particular cycles of training (yearly or *macrocycle,* monthly or *mezocycle,* and weekly or *microcycle*). Standard repetition of movements at maximal speed is necessary for developing speed, but it also leads to locking in speed at a certain level. With repetitive movements, the athlete's speed grows more slowly than the formation of a movement stereotype (in this instance a habit of moving with a certain, accustomed-to, speed). Such a movement stereotype or habit is called a *speed barrier.* This explains why so often, without regard for the amount of speed work performed, an athlete's sports achievement remains on the same level for several years. The firmly established speed barrier hinders realizing one's speed potential.

Speed exercises should be done right after the warm-up, at the beginning of the main part of a workout. In microcycles (weekly sequences of workouts) the workouts dedicated to speed are planned for the first or second day after the day of rest or after low intensity workouts. It is very important to properly plan tasks of speed training in a yearly cycle of training (macrocycle). With a foundation of good preparation by auxiliary and supplemental exercises, it is possible to reach the maximal speed—for a given level of training—during 6-8 weeks of sport-specific training.

Problems of sport-specific strength training and the perfection of skills are closely associated with the assigned workout tasks of speed development. If the maximal strength of a given individual increases, then his or her speed will increase in movements against great resistance but not in movements against little resistance. And conversely, increasing speed in movements with little or no external resistance leads to displaying greater velocities solely against little external resistance. For this reason, select only these exercises that increase speed in a sport-specific task or technique performed with the full amplitude of movements, including the form and timing of the technique and the rhythm of movements. Displaying speed is inseparably associated with technical perfection of movement. Proper technique permits the optimal use of one's physical fitness potential and thus a high effectiveness of actions.

### Training for Strength

*Strength is the ability to overcome external resistance or to oppose it through muscular effort. If we consider strength to be what in physics is called force, then in accordance with Newton's second law of dynamics, it is a product of mass and its acceleration.*

In developing jumping ability, one's acceleration determines the effectiveness of one's takeoff. So the task of strength exercises is to develop maximally fast muscle contraction balanced with an increase of tension. Such a form of strength is called *explosive strength* to stress its extremely dynamic character.

In developing strength according to the requirements of most sports, the coach or athlete will try to avoid excessive muscle build-up (hypertrophy). Building up muscles is the simplest way of increasing strength because strength displayed in a given movement depends on the sum of the surfaces of cross-sections of the muscle groups involved in this movement. In many sports this muscle building is "uneconomical" because it also increases the body mass that needs to be moved. Therefore strength training, taking into account natural changes of body mass that result from growing and maturing, is based mostly on perfecting neuromuscular coordination and lowering the threshold of activation of muscle motor units used in an athlete's techniques. Strength potential increases as a result of coordinating of muscle activity and synchronous mobilization of the greatest number of muscle fibers.

Generally strength training proceeds in three stages.

1. General strength training, which includes developing the strength of all muscle groups

2. Directed strength training, in which attention is on making muscles work in a way similar to that in one's sports discipline; at this stage the athlete forms a "functional strength foundation" specific for a given sport

3. Sport-specific strength training, consisting of developing the strength of those muscle groups that are the most active in the techniques of the sport, with simultaneous development of speed, while preserving the form and timing of the techniques of a given sport as fully as possible

At each of these stages there is an appropriate methodology of strength training, in accordance with the developmental potential of the athlete and the requirements of the sports discipline.

Practically, coaches and trainers call on a great number of exercises of different structure and character. Strength is developed mostly by exercises on apparatus or with barbells, dumbbells, and other equipment posing resistance that can be gradually changed with considerable precision. Sensible management of strength training divides all exercises into three groups.

1. General strength exercises, that is, various exercises affecting both the whole body and particular components that influence harmonious development of the whole person

2. Directed strength exercises, that is, various exercises affecting muscle groups directly and indirectly stressed in techniques of the sport, with the character (intensity and speed) of neuromuscular activity in those exercises similar to that in the techniques; the external structure (form of the movements) can be different than in actual techniques

3. Sport-specific strength exercises—the exercises that develop strength in association with speed of those muscles most engaged in the techniques of a given sport, within the same structure (form of movement) as in the sports techniques

At the stages of general and directed preparation, in strength training, two classic methods of performing resistance exercises are applied.

- **The repetitive method.** Exercises are repeated several times with the same intensity, while the character and duration of rest breaks are not set ahead of time but adjusted according to an athlete's fatigue; if the duration of rest breaks is fixed, then this will be the *interval method;* while performing a selected arrangement of exercises in fixed sequence and intensity for each makes it a *circuit method;*

- **The method of short maximal efforts.** An athlete moves from low resistance to nearly maximal resistance; for each workout, 3-5 different exercises are selected. An athlete starts each workout with resistance pegged at 30-40% of his or her result in the initial test of maximal training resistance.

In sport-specific training, joining the training of strength and speed while preserving the characteristic for a given sport structure of movements means that different methods apply. To develop simultaneously strength and speed in proportions close to those occurring in the technique requires a method of synthesizing influence.

In developing explosive strength, decreasing resistance while keeping the same intensity of effort will mainly develop its speed component. Increasing the resistance will develop its strength component. This way of training sport-specific strength is called the method of analytic influence.

To prevent creating a fixed movement habit, trainers in technical training should apply the method of differential influence, which involves performing technical exercises against various levels of resistance as fast as possible for each given amount of resistance.

Strength training for the majority of sports involves muscular efforts of mostly dynamic character, such as overcoming resistance (for example, vertical jumps) as well as movements that absorb loads (squatting down with a barbell, landing after jumping off a height).

The degree of resistance the athlete overcomes has an essential influence on the effectiveness of an exercise. External resistance may range from submaximal to small, it may be greater than that typically encountered during competition, equal to, or smaller than competition. Selection of the magnitude of resistance and of a point of reference— e.g., from the maximum of an athlete's strength potential, or from resistance typically occurring during competitions—depends on training goals, methods, and the athlete's experience.

Some equate the intensity of performance of a single exercise with the magnitude of resistance that has been overcome, but this is true only when the resistance is close to peak. The greatest possibility of changing the intensity of exercise occurs in exercises performed against small resistance (for example, vertical jumps with light weights). As in the case of the magnitude of resistance, intensity of a performed exercise can vary from maximal to low. It may also be greater than, equal to, or smaller than that typically encountered during competition. The goal of training determines the applied intensity. The greatest intensity of exercise can be achieved while overcoming resistance of 30-40% of one's maximal (life-record or absolute) resistance.

The number of sets depends on the method applied, but it should not exceed 60-70% of the maximal number of sets possible with the same rest breaks and constant intensity of exercise. Generally 2-6 sets are done for each exercise.

The number of repetitions in one set depends on the magnitude of resistance and the desired intensity of effort. With maximal resistance or extreme intensity, 1-2 repetitions are enough. In other cases 3-6 repetitions suffice, although sometimes (when stressing speed-endurance) the number of repetitions reaches 10.

Rest breaks last from 2 to 5 minutes depending on the goal of work, magnitude of resistance, intensity of efforts, and so on. Working against maximal resistance, or at extreme intensity, or with a high number of repetitions requires longer breaks. The first part of the rest break can have a passive character, but the remainder should be filled with loosening up movements.

Developing strength in its various forms (general, directed, sport-specific, short duration power) must be accomplished by the intensification of loads. Performing exercises in a prescribed time decides the effect of training to a greater degree than, for example, the spatial form of movements.

Many years' experience of developing explosive strength through squats and half-squats with a barbell shows that the greatest effects were obtained when an individual was held to strictly determined time limits within one set of 5 or 6 repetitions. It also turned out that such a program of exercises positively influences strength-endurance and sport-specific endurance. Thus the plan cannot be based solely on the total amount of work. There also needs to be a clear concept of intensifying this work. This follows from the goal of training, the athlete's skill level and experience, the training stage, and training cycle.

Having a set of methods for load control and the programmed intensification of work is the condition for effectively directing an athlete's training and working out new programs of training. Three effective methods tested in practice are recommended.

*1. An effective formula for training intensity in the whole preparatory period lies in distinguishing three zones of duration of exercises, as follows:*

- slow zone, duration of a set from more than 11.0 to 14.5 seconds;

- medium speed zone, duration of a set from more than 8.5 to 11.0 seconds;

- fast zone, duration of a set from 6.5 to 8.5 seconds.

Exercises are done in sets of 5 or 6 repetitions, starting with initial weight equaling 50% of one's maximum, and then increasing weight by 5 to 10 kg (11 to 22 lb.) in each next set.

Appropriate determination of the zones' durations is made by a coach, for example, through extending it by 1 second if the weight is very heavy.

Intensification of work during a workout in the preparatory period is based on moving on to the next, more intense zone of exercise duration when the athlete's improved shape warrants it. For example, the trainer can move the athlete from the slow zone to the medium speed zone, or from the medium to the fast zone, or through all three zones in succession. An example of weights used in the medium speed zone by four athletes is shown in figure 40. The principle demonstrated here is overcoming increasing loads in sets, within the zone's duration. If the duration for the zone is exceeded, the work with this exercise should be finished. In this manner every athlete performs work according to his or her individual capability of maintaining the assigned intensity.

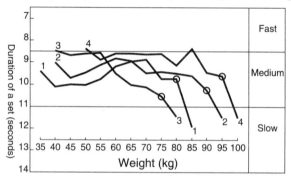

*Figure 40. Changes of duration of a set of five squats with a barbell with increasing weight, within the medium speed zone; numbers denote data of four different athletes*

2. *The second method is based on applying an individually determined intensity for each athlete, for each part—general and sport-specific—of the preparatory period.* Plans of intensity that incorporate graduated weight increases, are based on data from an initial trial conducted at the beginning of a given macrocycle (annual or semiannual training cycle). At that time the athlete performs 5 or 6 squats or half-squats with 50% of his or her maximum weight, at the maximal speed. To the obtained time one second (1 s) is added to ensure proper performance of no less than six sets of the selected exercise in a workout. This established duration for the set is not changed as the weight of the barbell increases. If the duration is exceeded (performance is too slow), the work with this exercise is finished in a given workout. With this approach the athlete strives to increase the number of sets of the exercise. If the athlete does not succeed during a given workout, he or she will attempt to do it during the next one. In this way the athlete is self-motivated to work more intensely. The data in tables 2 and 3 and figure 41 shows these principles applied.

As can be seen in table 2, during the first workout of the subperiod of sport-specific preparation, an athlete performing five squats with the barbell weighing 70 kg (154 lb.), at the maximal speed, took 5.6 seconds. After adding 1 second it was determined that, in subsequent workouts of this subperiod, the time of performing one set of this exercise should not be longer than 6.6 seconds. Exceeding this time indicates fatigue and the need to stop repeating the exercise. A record of five consecutive workouts is shown in table 2.

*Table 2. Sample changes of the time of performing five squats with barbell during sport-specific preparatory period*

| | Workout | Weight in kg | | | | | | | | |
|---|---|---|---|---|---|---|---|---|---|---|
| | | 70 | 75 | 80 | 85 | 90 | 95 | 100 | 105 | 110 |
| Duration of a set (in seconds) | 1 | 5.60▲ | 5.65 | 6.00 | 6.05 | 6.34 | 6.25 | 6.58t | 6.65 | – |
| | 2 | 5.95 | 5.72 | 5.90 | 6.11 | 6.35 | 6.55▼ | 6.75 | – | – |
| | 3 | 5.70 | 6.40 | 6.45 | 6.20 | 6.55 | 6.55 | 6.60▼ | 6.70 | – |
| | 4 | 5.60 | 5.60 | 5.80 | 5.70 | 6.10 | 6.40 | 6.50 | 6.55▼ | 6.80 |
| | 5 | 5.55 | 5.65 | 5.80 | 5.82 | 6.04 | 6.44 | 6.53 | 6.50▼ | 7.40 |

▲ *First workout—first set with weight of 70 kg (154 lb.) performed at maximal speed during 5.6 seconds, plus 1 second = 6.6 seconds, i.e., time determined for the whole subperiod*
▼ *Marks the last set before exceeding the time limit (6.6 seconds)*

The duration of another exercise—five half-squats with a barbell weighing 85 kg (187 lb.)— was determined in the identical manner. During the first workout (in the first set) the athlete performed the five half-squats within 5.4 seconds. After adding 1 second it was determined that, in subsequent workouts of this subperiod, the time for performing one set of this exercise should not be longer than 6.4 seconds. Exceeding this time would indicate fatigue and the need to stop repeating the exercise. A record of six consecutive workouts is shown in table 3 and figure 41.

*Table 3. Sample changes of the time of performing five half-squats with barbell during sport-specific preparatory period*

| | Work-out | Weight in kg | | | | | | | | | | | |
|---|---|---|---|---|---|---|---|---|---|---|---|---|---|
| | | 85 | 90 | 95 | 100 | 105 | 110 | 115 | 120 | 125 | 130 | 135 | 140 | 145 |
| Duration of a set (in seconds) | 1 | 5.40▲ | 5.45 | 5.48 | 5.62 | 5.90 | 5.85 | 6.30t | 6.48 | – | – | – | – | – |
| | 2 | 5.45 | 5.55 | 5.65 | 5.70 | 5.82 | 5.85 | 5.95 | 6.38▼ | 6.45 | – | – | – | – |
| | 3 | 5.70 | 5.75 | 5.70 | 5.80 | 5.80 | 5.90 | 5.97 | 6.00 | 6.20 | 6.38▼ | 6.47 | – | – |
| | 4 | 5.40 | 5.60 | 5.60 | 5.67 | 5.70 | 5.95 | 6.00 | 6.05 | 6.00 | 6.10 | 6.15 | 6.20▼ | 6.75 |
| | 5 | 5.30 | 5.55 | 5.50 | 5.60 | 5.67 | 5.70 | 5.90 | 5.85 | 6.35▼ | 6.70 | – | – | – |
| | 6 | 5.50 | 5.85 | 5.55 | 5.65 | 5.63 | 5.50 | 5.80 | 5.80 | 5.87 | 5.90 | 5.90 | 6.30▼ | 6.80 |

▲ *First workout—first set with weight of 85 kg (187 lb.) performed at maximal speed during 5.4 seconds, plus 1 second = 6.4 seconds, i.e., time determined for the whole subperiod*
▼ *Marks the last set before exceeding the time limit (6.4 seconds)*

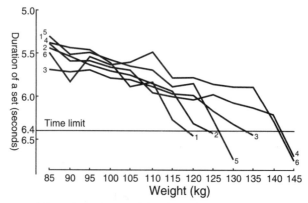

*Figure 41. Changes of duration of a set of five half-squats with a barbell with increasing weight; numbers denote data from different workouts; time norm for performing the exercise (6.4 seconds) was set at the first workout*

3. The third method is based on *individually planning a strictly determined intensity for each athlete during each workout.* As athletic condition improves, the necessity of individualizing training loads assigned for each workout shows itself. Table 4 (page 16) shows strictly determined norms of intensity of work on the basis of maximal speed of performing the first set of squats before the main part of each workout. For example, a set of five repetitions with a barbell weighing 60 kg (132 lb.) took 5.95 seconds during the first workout (figure 42). Adding a 1 second margin, it was determined that during this workout the time of performing a set of five repetitions of squats should not exceed 6.95 seconds. If it did exceed the set limit, further performing of this work was stopped. During the next workout, the new time norm for this exercise is determined in the same way. That the methods proposed here are warranted is confirmed by the data presented in table 5 (page 17). Practical examples are shown in figures 43, 44, and 45 (pages 15-16).

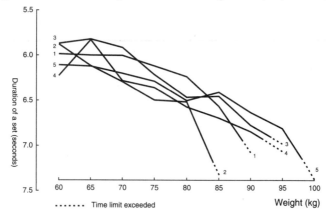

*Figure 42. Changes of duration of a set of five squats with a barbell during five consecutive workouts; time norms for performing the exercise were set at the beginning of each workout*

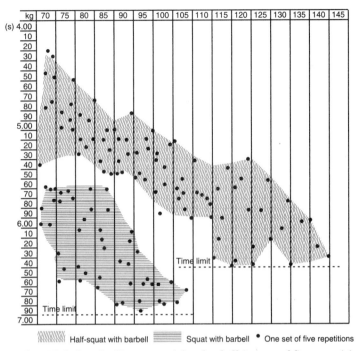

*Figure 43. Athlete M.J. does half-squats with a barbell in sets of five repetitions each up to maximal weight within the time limit of 6.4 seconds (examples from seven workouts); squats with barbell in sets of five repetitions each up to maximal weight within a time limit of 6.9 seconds (examples from seven workouts)*

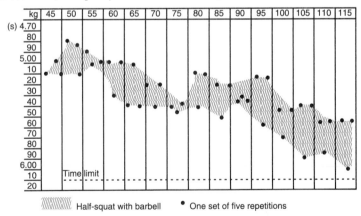

*Figure 44. Athlete I.S. does half-squats with a barbell in sets of five repetitions each up to maximal weight within the time limit of 6.1 seconds (examples from three workouts); progressing in subsequent sets of five repetitions each up to maximal weight; time limit determined on the basis of test in initial set plus 1 second*

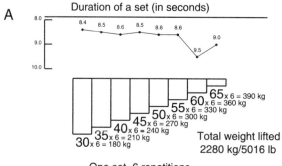

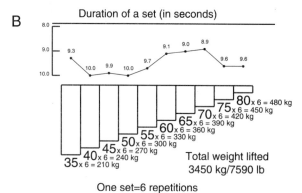

*Figure 45. Athlete J.J. does squats with barbell in the zone of medium speed: A—initial test; B—test after 40 workouts*

*Table 4. Sample changes of the time of performing five squats with a barbell, with time norms determined for each workout*

| | Work-out | Time of an initial set with 60 kg | Time norm for the exercise | Weight in kg | | | | | | | |
|---|---|---|---|---|---|---|---|---|---|---|---|
| | | | | 65 | 70 | 75 | 80 | 85 | 90 | 95 | 100 |
| Dura-tion of a set (in sec-onds) | 1 | 5.95 | 6.95 | 5.98 | 5.97 | 6.10 | 6.20 | 6.53▼ | 7.00 | – | – |
| | 2 | 5.85 | 6.85 | 5.80 | 6.25 | 6.45 | 6.46 | 6.40 | 6.75▼ | 6.95 | – |
| | 3 | 5.85 | 6.85 | 6.10 | 6.25 | 6.32 | 6.53 | 6.66 | 6.80▼ | 7.00 | – |
| | 4 | 6.20 | 7.20 | 5.80 | 5.90 | 6.20 | 6.50▼ | 7.30 | – | – | – |
| | 5 | 6.10 | 7.10 | 6.10 | 6.20 | 6.25 | 6.50 | 6.38 | 6.60 | 6.80▼ | 7.30 |

▼ *Marks the last set before exceeding the time limit*

*Table 5. Samples of tests after working through one preparatory period with Polish triple jumpers*

| Athlete | Strength fitness | Jumping fitness |
|---|---|---|
| | squat with barbell, increase of the barbell's weight compared to the initial test (kg) | 5-jump without a prerun, from left foot to right foot, increase of the distance compared to the initial test (cm) |
| M.J. | +25.00 | +177.00 |
| J.J. | +30.00 | + 75.00 |
| A.I. | +25.00 | +106.00 |
| R.G. | +25.00 | +117.00 |
| E.O. | +40.00 | + 45.00 |
| P.B. | +25.00 | +105.00 |
| A.T. | +16.00 | + 72.00 |
| Average | +26.42 | + 99.57 |

What are the tasks of strength training in a yearly training cycle?

In the general part of the preparatory period—the task is regaining the level of strength possessed at the end of the previous sport-specific preparatory period.

In the sport-specific part of the preparatory period, the goal is to increase strength to a new, higher level.

During the competition period, the athlete must maintain the level of strength achieved during the preparatory period.

In the transition period, the trainer will not allow the athlete's strength to decrease significantly.

So, in training for strength there are three tasks—developing strength, maintaining it, and rebuilding it to a previously achieved level. Development requires most work, maintenance the least. The trainer must keep the athlete from squandering his or her previously achieved strength.

It is also important to control indicators of how strength and speed relate in particular periods of a yearly training cycle. Essential information on this subject is supplied by an analysis of correlations between the results of strength tests with the results of tests of other aspects of an athlete's fitness preparation. Most strength exercises within a training program are applied in the general preparatory period. In the sport-specific preparatory period, strength exercises take on a sport-specific character. The amount of work on strength decreases, but its intensity increases. In competitive periods strength exercises are applied solely for maintaining the achieved level of strength.

## Training for Jumping Ability

*Jumping ability enables athlete to move like a ball or a spring. A high level of jumping ability is the final result of speed-strength training.*

Jumping ability exercises are very dynamic, they mobilize all muscle groups and organize their actions, they are a functional result of speed and strength, and they demand good coordination. Selecting an appropriate combination of terrain, conditions, and exercises with suitable resistance makes it possible for these exercises to be an effective part of a training program at any stage of an athlete's career.

Seven groups of exercises constitute training for jumping ability.

1. Jumping exercises in a spot, performed in series, are an effective means of developing explosive strength and other abilities of the neuromuscular system, such as a sense of space, of rhythm, balance, proprioception, movement coordination, and agility. These exercises do not require apparatus, are easy to perform, and are exciting. A series consists of 5 exercises, and each of these exercises is repeated 8-10 times. Here is an example of such a series.

Exercise 1. 10 jumps off both feet over an obstacle (for, example, a ball)
Exercise 2. 10 jumps off left foot in a spot
Exercise 3. 10 jumps off right foot in a spot
Exercise 4. 10 jumps off both feet, from a squat, over an obstacle (for example, a ball)
Exercise 5. 10 reach jumps to a suspended ball, alternating take-off foot

During the rest breaks between series, athletes perform flexibility exercises, relaxing movements, and jog. Ten minutes is dedicated to each series of exercises. Beginners are advised to include jumping ability exercises within the main part of workout, while advanced athletes can do them within the last part of a warm-up.

**2. Jumps with a prerun.** Here are included track-and-field jumps and gymnastic jumps. In all these exercises, performed one at a time, in various conditions (height, takeoff spot, kind of takeoff, and so on), the trainer can also impose additional movements or tasks that develop coordination.

**3. Flat [for distance] multijumps**—from standing still and with a prerun, these are mainly jumps from foot to foot, with alternating arm movements, performed at distances of 10-50 meters (33-165 feet) with various tasks, for example, 5-10 jumps for the greatest distance, or covering a distance of 30-40 meters (99-132 feet) with the least number of jumps, or performing the most jumps at a distance of 50-60 meters (165-198 feet) within an assigned time. In all these exercises the takeoff is directed forward, thrusting the other leg forward (and not up). The athlete should stress a grabbing motion with the foot immediately upon landing—the ball of the foot should actively pull the ground. In these jumps softness, elasticity, and a rhythmic quality of movements are essential. They are performed in sets, after which the athlete ought to do light runs with increasing velocity and control of the technique of running. The distance the athlete covers with a set of jumps and how many times this distance is repeated depends on the athlete's experience.

These multijumps develop strength of the muscle extensors of legs. For advanced athletes it is advisable to occasionally apply resistance to the thigh (weighted strips of 150-200 grams [5.25 oz.-7 oz.]) or to the waist (belt weighing 2-3 kg [4.4 lb.-6.6 lb.]). Exercises of this type are done in the main part of a workout.

**4. Multijumps over obstacles**—from standing still and with a prerun. This group of exercises comprises jumps over obstacles (medicine balls, hurdles, segments of gymnastic vault boxes) from single-leg and two-leg takeoff. The jumps are done from standing still and with a prerun, in sets of 5-20 takeoffs. Very often exercises of this type are assembled into "obstacle courses" with obstacles of various heights and varying distances between subsequent obstacles. Such exercises are done in the main part of the workout. Besides jumping ability they also improve coordination.

**5. Depth jumps.** These exercises are associated with high, so-called reactive muscular tensions, and are very stressful on the joints. Exercises of this type ought to be used only by experienced athletes, well-prepared in the course of long-term training. These jumps are performed one at a time or combined into series of 3-6 jumps with intermediate jumps up on top of an obstacle of 20-100 cm (8" to 40"). The total number of jumps within one workout should not exceed 30 jumps. Advanced athletes can periodically apply a small external resistance. During a workout depth jumps are done together with other jumping exercises. They are very intense and an effective means of developing jumping ability.

**6. Jumps and situational jumping tasks.** These exercises are done mainly outdoors, while negotiating natural obstacles (fallen trees, ditches, bushes, and so on). It is also possible to arrange an appropriately varied obstacle course in a stadium or a gym. Such a course then would have to be negotiated several times, with rest breaks filled with, for example, flexibility exercises. This kind of training perfects movement coordination to a considerable degree because during subsequent workouts the trainer can change the kind and sequence of obstacles as well as conditions for surmounting them.

**7. Sport-specific technical exercises.** These are exercises of a given sport based on jumping ability, for example, basketball's or team handball's jumping shot, jumping block or spike in volleyball, intercepting a high ball with the head in soccer. Such exercises, either in the form of a full technique or of its part, perfect jumping ability.

Jumping ability exercises can aim to develop either higher speed or strength. Which is accomplished depends on directing the athlete to concentrate either on speed of movements or on muscle tension. The chosen goal can also be forced by an appropriate arrangement of an obstacle course or by adding weights such as a belt, vest, or an inner tube filled with sand. Selection of exercises and the conditions for performing them are determined mainly by requirements of the sport and an athlete's experience and fitness potential.

Within a training program, jumping exercises (especially groups 1-4 and 6) play a particularly important role at the stage of general fitness preparation, when because of developmental considerations it is not advisable to use strength exercises with substantial external resistance.

Advanced athletes often combine jumping exercises with other forms of exercises.

## Developing Ability to Control Movements

Speed-strength training is the foundation for an athlete's dynamic actions. These dynamic actions are complex movements that require precise control and that depend on such abilities as flexibility, coordination, the ability to relax muscles, and a sense of rhythm. These abilities enable actions properly exercising speed-strength abilities according to the requirements of technique.

*Flexibility is the ability to perform movements of great amplitude and refers to movement of the whole skeleton and skeletal musculature; referring to a given joint, we speak of its* mobility. Flexibility to a large extent depends on the elasticity of muscles and tendons. The elasticity of muscles can change under the influence of contest conditions or an athlete's emotional state. When performing flexibility exercises, one should consider changes caused by temperature and the time of the day. On cold and humid days, when flexibility can decrease, the intensity of the warm-up should be increased.

Too many strength exercises can decrease mobility of the joints. A rational combination of flexibility exercises with strength exercises leads to a high degree of development of both these abilities (Balsevich and Zaporozhanov 1987, Verkhoshansky 1988). The best results in developing flexibility are achieved by beginning appropriate exercises between the ages of 10 and 14, with full potential reached around 15-16.

In the long-term training program, the process of developing flexibility can be divided into three stages.

1) Joints' gymnastics

2) Sport-specific development of joint mobility

3) Maintaining mobility of joints at the achieved level

The task of the first stage, apart from increasing mobility of all joints, is also strengthening them.

The second stage has as its goal the development of maximal freedom of movement where that range of movement helps technique and thus improves sports results.

The third stage—the stage of maintaining mobility of joints—is about doing flexibility exercises for the rest of an athlete's career. There can be relatively large changes in the amount of these exercises depending on the athlete's needs at the time.

The necessity for systematic flexibility training is predicated on the amount of time needed for developing passive mobility up to 90% of what is anatomically possible, for:

- spine joints—up to 60 days,

- hip joints—from 60 to 120 days,

- knee joints—up to 30 days,

- ankle joints—up to 30 days.

Among exercises that increase the passive mobility of joints are the following.

- Passive movements performed with partner's assistance

- Passive movements performed with weights

- Passive movements performed with the help of springs

- Static exercises in which positions of maximal stretch are held for 3 to 6 seconds

Here are exercises that develop active mobility of joints.

- Swings and circular movements of limbs and trunk

- Leans and extensions (of the trunk or neck, for example)

- Other stretches, such as deep lunges

Active mobility of joints can also be developed with resistance exercises, such as these.

- Weight exercises

- Exercises against partner's resistance

- Exercises against elastic resistance (for example, of springs or bungee cords)

Flexibility exercises should be done together with loosening up exercises. Advanced athletes should do more repetitions of flexibility exercises than beginners, as the following table suggests.

*Table 6. Flexibility exercise repetitions*

| Flexibility exercise | Number of repetitions for beginners | Number of repetitions for advanced |
|---|---|---|
| for knee | up to 20 | 25 |
| for spine | up to 60 | 100 |
| for hip | up to 50 | up to 70 |

Muscles should be relaxed before performing flexibility exercises. Stretching is a good injury prevention. The better prepared are the muscles, the greater is the range of motion and the less the risk of injury (straining muscles or tendons).

Flexibility is developed by performing exercises requiring an increasing range of movements. Attempts to increase range in a single exercise give little effect. Repeating the exercises leads to an accumulation of their effects, which gives increased range. This is why stretching exercises should be done in sets of a few repetitions each. During a workout, stretching exercises can be done until a light pain is felt. This is a sign to stop stretching. The greatest effect of stretching exercises is achieved by doing them twice every day. At the stage of maintaining mobility (i.e., when the desired level of flexibility has already been reached), flexibility exercises can be done every other or every third day. Flexibility exercises can be assigned to athletes as homework. During a workout these exercises are included in the warm-up or in the main part.

Flexibility exercises should always be preceded by a thorough warm-up. Increased range of motion resulting from static passive flexibility exercises lasts briefly (10-12 minutes at room temperature). Lessening the heat loss (through warm clothes) can extend this time. After exercises including active movements, increased flexibility lasts longer than after exercises with passive movements.

Within fitness preparation flexibility plays an important role. The trainer must guard against overdoing training for flexibility and the development of mobility in joints. Excessively stretched muscles and joints that are too mobile do not help with sports results, and can cause injuries and difficulties in mastering the proper technique.

Flexibility exercises have as their goals preparing the body for competition and mastering effective technique. Development of flexibility is thus tied closely to perfecting movement coordination (neuromuscular coordination).

*Coordination is the ability to perform complex movements, switching from one set of complex movements to another, and also is the ability to react quickly to an unexpected situation with the sometimes new but in any case most appropriate movement.* The concept of movement coordination is diverse and ambiguous. From a practical point of view it is the sum of adroit movements of the whole body and manual dexterity, mainly hand-eye coordination. Coordination depends on many factors, including movement talent, experience, imagination, and movement memory. Because each new skill is at least somewhat formed from previously learned elements, the greater the athlete's store of skills the less trouble he or she has with mastering new ones. So, the basic method of perfecting coordination is to introduce new, diverse exercises continuously, while also performing the already known ones (including one's techniques) in different and changing conditions.

To perfect coordination, use the following groups of exercises.

• Exercises perfecting maintenance of balance in static positions and in motion

• Exercises developing the skill of performing quick turns and rolls

- Exercises with asymmetric movements

- Exercises with atypical initial positions

- Exercises with unusual movements added to their normal form

- Exercises in atypical conditions

Because coordination exercises cause fatigue relatively quickly, while their effectiveness depends on a precise sensing of space and time (which requires being fresh), they are conducted according to the repetitive method with appropriately long rest breaks. In workouts combining more than one type of exercise, the coordination exercises are placed in the first part of the workout. In the yearly training cycle the order of using coordination exercises is as follows.

- In periods of the general preparation—learning various new exercises, including those far removed from one's sport

- In periods of sport-specific preparation—applying a wide variety of sport-specific exercises

- In the first halves of competition periods—training of various versions of technique

- In the second halves of competition periods—perfecting a selected version of the techniques in changing conditions

The repertoire of coordination exercises should be systematically changed by introducing new exercises or new tasks in known exercises. For these exercises to serve their purpose, as soon as proficiency with their form is achieved, the athlete must strive for maximally fast performance and the ability to combine them with technical tasks. For example, a boxer might have to jump and rotate along his vertical axis and immediately upon landing assume a fighting stance and throw a combination of punches.

Training of coordination should be done continuously, because if no new exercises are introduced over a long period of time, the athlete's ability to learn new skills decreases. The goal is not the utmost mastery of new skills but just proficiency with the general form of exercise (Vierkhoshanskiy 1988).

Very closely associated with speed and flexibility and also with movement coordination is *the ability to relax muscles.* Sports training leads to increasing the difference between muscle tonus at the highest and the lowest effort. Increasing the difference between maximum effort and rest is beneficial because it increases the capability of maintaining maximal pace of movements. The skill of relaxing muscles in various conditions is essential if the athlete is to improve his or her competitive results. The athlete begins to learn these skills initially while performing special exercises dedicated solely to relaxing the muscles, later during the workout, and ultimately during the contest (Grosser and Starischka 1989).

Flexibility training has an indirect influence on muscle relaxation, but alone is not enough. Here are the basic means of developing the skill of relaxing muscles.

- Special exercises such as the "bicycle" (legs make pedaling movements in the air) performed at a moderate pace while lying on one's neck and shoulders; rapid vibration of the limbs; self-massage—especially rubbing, kneading, and shaking; gentle swinging on the bar; or rocking while curled into a ball

- Sauna or hot bath (38-40° C [100.4-104° F])

- Relaxing positions, lowering mental tension through yoga exercises, turning off the consciousness, and so on.

Every exercise has its own characteristic *rhythm of movement* in its sequence of phases and links within the movement chain. Particular phases and links have various functions but are all subordinated to the effectiveness of the whole movement. The problem of the proper rhythm—very important for manifesting speed—in acyclic exercises is considered within a framework of technique and neuromuscular coordination.

Rhythm determines the conditions of manifesting speed and permits full utilization of technical skills. Exercises performed smoothly, preserving a proper rhythm of particular phases and accentuation of crucial links of the movement chain, ensure the highest—at a given stage of training—speed of performance. Perfecting rhythm has essential associations with coordination, flexibility, and technique; it is also influenced by the strength of muscle groups involved in a given movement.

Here are principles of developing flexibility, coordination, relaxation, and keeping proper rhythm. Perfecting all these abilities must be subordinated to the tasks of mastering effective technique and utilizing one's full potential. Only then is it possible to achieve cohesion of fitness preparation.

## Endurance Preparation as a Foundation of Training

*Despite appearances endurance is a necessary component of fitness preparation in virtually all sports. Endurance is the ability to perform prolonged effort at the required intensity, while maintaining sufficient effectiveness of actions without succumbing to fatigue in efforts occurring in various external conditions.* There are two kinds of endurance: *general* and *sport-specific*. In reference to a particular stage of training or selection of exercises, the term *directed endurance* is used.

**General endurance** is the ability to perform, for a long time, any physical effort that engages most muscle groups. An adequate level of endurance makes it possible to train at a specified degree of difficulty and load. Training for general endurance is conducted mostly in the general preparatory period.

**Directed endurance** is based on general endurance and serves as a transition stage for sport-specific training (for example, endurance directed to jumping ability).

**Sport-specific endurance** is the ability to overcome a sport-specific load for the time required by the conditions of competition. This form of endurance is associated with the specific demands of a given sport discipline. Joining requirements of fitness and of technique, it makes possible the keeping up of an adequate effort for the whole duration of the workout or contest, which ultimately leads to a high sports result.

Training for general endurance consists mainly of various forms of terrain-running workouts and *fartlek* (speed play), as well as appropriate forms of circuit training. The athlete must also develop an association of endurance with other abilities (for example, endurance-jumping ability, endurance-strength).

Developing general endurance consists first of all in improving function of the cardio-vascular and respiratory systems, ensuring the efficient functioning of the athlete. Exercising takes the form of methods and means similar to these of runners, not so much and not so intense, but with a greater concentration on speed-strength exercises.

Training for running in conjunction with the parallel training of other movement abilities leads to developing great shape, perfects a sense of rhythm, and strengthens joints and ligaments. Endurance training conducted throughout the whole preparatory period in varied terrain, in various weather also develops the traits of will and mental toughness.

For sports events in which endurance is not a decisive ability, the fundamental forms of developing general endurance are terrain workouts and fartlek.

**Terrain-running workouts** are the easiest and the least stressing means of developing endurance. The length of distances run is not specified, and neither is the time and character of rest breaks. From marching interspersed with jogging, athletes progress to more intensive varieties of running (light runs, running up a slope, skips, accelerations) alternated with rest while marching.

In its full form a terrain-running workout includes 3-6 repetitions of a moderately paced run for 200 meters (655 feet). All repetitions are run at the same speed, and without pronounced fatigue. In this type of workout attention is on the proper technique of running and on introducing tasks that develop movement abilities other than endurance.

Terrain-running workouts are used with beginners as well as with advanced athletes, in which case it is used mostly in the general preparatory period. Such workouts accustom the athlete to the effort of running. Workouts are done once a week, best during daylight, for 60-75 minutes.

**Fartlek** (speed play) is best for the fullest development of general endurance. It is introduced after terrain-running workouts have accustomed the athlete to running. The magnitude of efforts gradually increases. The number and quality of exercises are specified and constitute the measure of an athlete's effort. The sequence of doing particular exercises is also specified. Fartlek consists of four parts.

**Part 1, introductory.** This first part has a goal of accustoming an athlete to intensive effort through adaptation of the circulatory and respiratory systems as well as warming up muscles and joints. It ends with flexibility and agility exercises.

**Part 2, speed and jumping exercises.** The exercises of part 2 are done in continuous motion. Distances are run at a lively pace with full looseness and large range of movements.

**Part 3, running endurance.** This part requires covering distances of 300-150 meters (984-492 feet) 4-6 times—the same distance each time—at an easy pace that depends on the athletes' endurance. In later workouts distances shorten so at the end of the preparatory period the athlete is running sets between 120 and 150 meters (393 to 492 feet), again, the same distance each time. While the distances shortens, the speed increases. It is necessary to individualize the speed and the duration of rest breaks. Athletes of strong constitution, of strong build, should run longer distances for greater economy and looseness of movements. For those of long limbs and slim musculature, who have a greater natural looseness, shorter distances run at a faster pace will suffice.

The character and duration of rest breaks depends on the athlete's experience and condition. Beginners rest during light movement or a jog until their breathing calms down. A rest break for advanced athletes consists of 2 to 4 minutes of continuous movement, until their pulse rate returns to about 120 beats per minute.

**Part 4, calming down and relaxing.** This part consists of calming and relaxing activities. (See pages 23-24 for examples of relaxation techniques.)

A necessary condition for fully developing an athlete's movement coordination and fitness is conducting the fartlek in rolling terrain, or at least diverse, using natural obstacles, springy ground, deep snow, and so on.

Endurance training is a component of fitness preparation. Besides the terrain runs and fartlek, general training of other movement abilities also contributes to the development of endurance. Obstacle courses indoors and outdoors, various arrangements of circuit training, ball games, and appropriately applied other sports all play an important role. Progression is from the mildest exercises, applied often, to the most strenuous, applied with mature athletes once a week, in some such strict form as fartlek, for example. This principle holds for the whole preparatory period.

The level of endurance, achieved in the course of the preparatory period, added to the development of other abilities associated with fitness preparation, allows the athlete to train with sport-specific tasks that increase year after year. Each method and form of endurance training used causes specific functional changes in the athlete's body. The relationship of the particular components determines the character of a training unit (workout, microcycle, period), developing the respective form of endurance. Choice of exercises (general, directed, or sport-specific) plays the principal role depending on the stage and training period.

The first part of preparatory period is dedicated to increasing the general fitness of the athlete through a high volume of training with pronounced oscillations of intensity. The second part of the preparatory period is directed toward developing sport-specific endurance through the growing use of means and methods of sport-specific training. The foundation for endurance preparation is a proper program of work during out-of-season training.

During the period of sport-specific preparation and the competition period, endurance manifests itself mainly in its sport-specific form. It has a very close connection with the technical training of a given sport. A high level of sport-specific endurance is built by performing workouts with a high volume of sport-specific work in yearly and weekly cycles (microcycles) of training, exceeding even competitive loads. As a rule, in a period when competitions are done once every week, one workout in the middle of the week should be dedicated to endurance training. Nevertheless, between series of competitions the main stress is always on rebuilding sport-specific endurance.

A methodology for endurance training ought to have these goals.

- Developing the ability to perform intensive efforts during competition even though experiencing fatigue (before the appearance of the signs of fatigue)

- Developing resilience and readiness for effectively solving competitive tasks

- Constantly raising the level of the basic components of sport-specific endurance and optimizing their interrelations

- Economization of muscle actions in sport-specific efforts

One important way to develop sport-specific endurance is to participate in competitions throughout the sport-specific preparation period while observing this principle: Work up from less important competitions to more important.

## Control of Training

Control of training always refers to a specific athlete, and the coach or trainer must be concerned with immediate, delayed, and cumulative training effects. *Immediate training effect* relates to the condition of the athlete at the end of a just-executed exercise, series of exercises, or a workout. For example, it manifests itself as the athlete's raised heart rate, breathing rate, and temperature. *Delayed training effect* relates to the athlete's condition some hours after a workout. It is what the immediate training effect becomes with the passage of more time since the end of the workout. The degree of an athlete's body recovery and rebuilding between workouts relates to this delayed training effect. Finally, *cumulative training effect* is more long-range, representing the results of all the delayed training effects. Coaches and trainers typically measure the effects of a whole training cycle or period on the athlete's skills and abilities to picture the cumulative training effect. The level of fitness, as initially determined, ought to serve as the basis for elaborating training programs for subsequent stages—of general preparation, directed preparation, sport-specific preparation—and particular training cycles.

The effectiveness of training work is determined by a few factors, principal among which are selection of training loads with regard to their type, volume, and intensity. As the athlete's body adapts to applied loads, they no longer lead to further progress, so the main problem of training boils down to finding a way of continuously intensifying these loads.

Where the athlete is in this process of adapting must be evaluated and anticipated by the coach, so the coach must have some means of control. This applies mainly to the training of athletes of the highest caliber, because the great loads undertaken by them can (and very often do) lead to overloading, and even overtraining. On the other hand, not challenging the athletes with loads—too low for their level—may cause a loss of training time for the lack of effects. The basis for planning and control of training intensity ought to be an analysis of the athlete's current state of conditioning and results of tests from the previous year (or training cycle).

Development of athletic form depends on perfecting methods of control of the current loads and planning of future ones. Only on the basis of data from control is it possible to optimize the training process.

For example, an athlete's strength deficiencies in sport-specific actions determine what exercises should be his or her focus.

If an athlete has good results in a reach jump done from standing still, but exhibits a long support phase during takeoff in his or her sports technique, this situation calls for plyometrics. Plyometrics shorten the time of switching from an eccentric muscle action (a landing or a stomp preceding a takeoff) to a concentric action of the takeoff itself.

Poor results in a reach jump done from standing still indicate low explosive strength, especially if an athlete's maximal strength in a squat (as measured by maximal weight lifted) is high. Short sets of squats and half-squats performed very fast develop explosive strength.

## Directions of Jumping Ability and Explosive Strength Training

A systemic understanding of physical fitness incorporates jumping ability and explosive strength, conforming to the requirements of the model of mastery in a given sport discipline. This model changes from one training stage to next and one year to the next. The position and methods of jumping ability training can be pictured in the form of a "highway" leading from developing the speed-strength potential to attaining the highest sports results. (See fig. 1 on page 29.) This path has to be optimized, greatest effectiveness and efficiency sought, while always remembering that jumping ability training is only a part of a complex, systemic process. There must be no "shortcuts," no skipping stages of work that prepare for successive, increasingly sport-specific tasks (Sozanski and Sledziewski 1989).

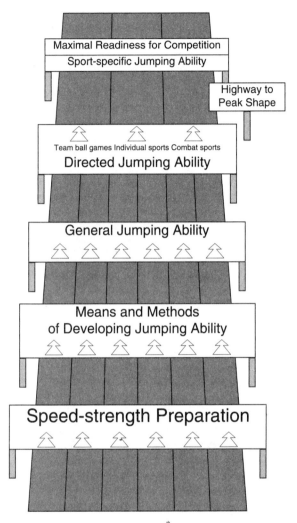

*Figure 1. Directions of jumping ability training*[*]

---

[*] See the note from the translator on page 2 regarding the terms "jumping ability training" and "explosive strength." Jumping ability is a manifestation of explosive strength in the form of a jump. Examples of other manifestations of explosive strength are punches or the arm action in shot put. Whenever the authors describe principles of jumping ability training, they mean also explosive strength training.

# 2

# Developing Jumping Ability in Stages of Sports Training

## Developing Jumping Ability in a Yearly Training Cycle

The model of development of jumping ability shown in figure 2 is a result of many years of practical experience. The model works for developing jumping ability for most sports.

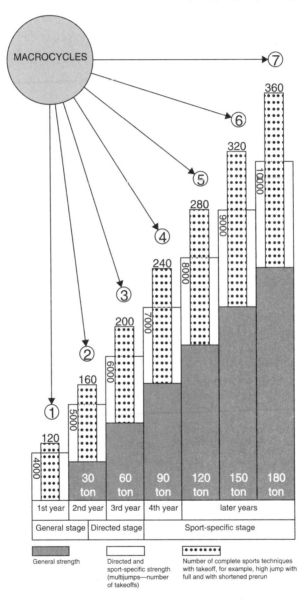

*Figure 2. Model of developing jumping ability in macrocycles for various stages of training*

The long-term plan presented here consists of seven macrocycles (yearly training cycles). It can be used for planning the pace of development of jumping ability in stages of sports training, for example, from a macrocycle for youth (macrocycle 1), without heavy resistance, to macrocycles with great loads and heavy resistance for high level athletes.

As mentioned previously, a prerequisite of jumping ability is a high level of strength, so for each of seven macrocycles appropriate proportions of work are proposed for general, directed, and sport-specific strength. The choice of a suitable macrocycle and applied training loads is determined by the stage of an athlete's development and the specific needs of a given sport with respect to jumping ability. The idea of this approach is to match load and exercise selection with properties of the structures of microcycles, mezocycles, and macrocycles typical for a given sport discipline.

The starting point for general preparation, which precedes the development of jumping ability, is a squat and a half-squat with extra weight or without. (Without weight, squats or half-squats would be jumps.)

Work on directed and sport-specific strength is based mainly on multijumps. These are the natural and the most effective exercises for developing jumping ability together with movement coordination.

## Rotation of Means of Training During Yearly Cycle

*Means of training* include exercises, facilities, apparatus, and equipment. The effectiveness of jumping ability development at all stages of training cannot result from chance. It is an outcome of well-planned training—selection of loads and methods and, most importantly, the system of varying and altering the means of training. Variety keeps exercises from becoming rigidly patterned after many years of repeating them with the same rhythm and intensity. Training of strength and jumping ability is integrally connected with coordination and technique exercises. The goal is a systematic enrichment of movement skills, necessary for improving results in competition. The effectiveness of training in many sports demands developing the ability of altering movement coordination. This is done through the introduction of novelty—new exercises, or in ball games introducing new tactics that might surprise potential opponents (Zglinicki 1993).

A high level of jumping ability combines strength, speed, and coordination, and so this ability is an inseparable part of training not only in preparatory periods, but also in preparation immediate to the competition, especially in ball games. In the process of training it is necessary to systematically change exercises, controlling their intensity and performance not only in training cycles of varying length (microcycle, mezocycle, macrocycle), but also in every workout.

A rotation within three groups of exercises (figure 3) is effective.

1) Dominant exercises, aimed toward realizing the goal of training at each period of the macrocycle

2) Auxiliary exercises, of general, directed, or sport-specific character, that can be rotated according to the needs of jumping ability training

3) Preventive exercises, aimed toward preventing injuries to ankle and knee joints during jumping ability training, varied according to the needs of the sport

| | Preparatory Period | | Competitive Period | Transition Period |
|---|---|---|---|---|
| General Preparation | Directed Preparation | Sport-specific Preparation | | |

Multijumps

Techniques of takeoff

The main task of the transition period is rest and preventing a drastic decline in strength.

Dominant exercises

Auxiliary exercises

Preventive exercises

*Figure 3. Rotation of exercises within three groups*

Using such a rotation model, it is permissible to repeat exercises in those cases where the coach has a poor store of training means, but only if he or she changes their character and intensity. Examples of such possibilities are shown in figures 4 and 5, each illustrating several changes of one exercise. Varying the coach's means of training systematically facilitates the effective development of jumping ability for various techniques and requirements of various sports.

1.    2.    3.    4.    5.    6.    7.    8.

*Figure 4. Example of several changes of an exercise—squat with and without weights*

*Figure 5. Example of several changes of an exercise—snatch*

## Multijumps—Natural Jumping Ability Exercises

Current trends for shortening the preparatory period result from the constant extending of the competition period. This forces coaches to make changes in planning with a view to prolonged high intensity training and prolonged maintenance of competitive form. Maintaining and building strength in cycles shorter but of greater intensity, requires the coach to take a new, efficient and imaginative approach. Helpful here are exercises for developing explosive strength, which make it possible to limit the need for strength exercises with heavy equipment such as a barbell (Starzynski 1987).

Multijumps are the most common means of developing jumping ability in nearly all sports. They are most effective for converting general strength to explosive strength. Their great value lies in teaching, in a natural way, the technique of takeoff in combination with sport-specific coordination of movements in time and space. This is the foundation for developing sport-specific forms of jumping ability, differing so much in every sport. Considering these properties, the full range of multijumps is shown on pages 58-101, in sets of exercises for particular groups of sports (individual, team ball games, and combat sports).

Another advantage of multijumps is that they can be used to develop agility and sport-specific strength, as well as jumping ability endurance. Multijumps, along with depth jumps, help to develop power of short duration—so much needed in contemporary training (Mroczynski and Starzynski 1994). The functional versatility of multijumps is further testified to by noting that in the sport-specific preparatory period (and during the competition period too) they can be used as auxiliary exercises for perfecting the technique of takeoff in virtually every sport. Multijumps are practiced mainly on grass or other elastic surfaces, or in snow of 20-80 cm (8-31 inches) depth. Control tests can be performed on an artificial track surface such as Tartan Turf.

In the general preparatory period, multijumps can be done with extra weights. This is not recommended as the competition period gets nearer, however, because it can adversely affect coordination and the precision of the athlete's takeoff technique.

### Long-term sequence of applying multijumps

- Multijumps on soft surface, no prerun

- Multijumps in deep snow (20-80 cm [8-31 inches]), no prerun

- Multijumps on soft surface, including prerun

- Multijumps in deep snow (20-80 cm [8-31 inches]), including prerun

All multijumps with or without a prerun should be performed in an accelerating rhythm. The longer the prerun, the more intense the jumps. Intensification of multijumps happens by appropriate shortening of their distance, reducing the number of takeoffs.

### Kinds of multijumps

- From left foot to right foot, no prerun

- From left foot to right foot, with a prerun

- From left foot to left foot again, then to right foot, no prerun

- From left foot to left foot again, then to right foot, with a prerun

- On one foot, no prerun

- On one foot, with a prerun

- On both feet together, no prerun

- On both feet together, with a prerun

- On both feet together over obstacles (hurdles, for example), no prerun

- On both feet together over obstacles, with a prerun

- On one foot over obstacles, no prerun

- On one foot over obstacles, with a prerun

The athlete should end all multijumps with a landing in a sand box or some other soft and safe place or, if there is to be no landing, with a slow run. Also, he or she will use different multijumps in the workout.

Table 1 presents examples of the number of jumps and takeoffs in a workout dedicated to developing jumping ability, with choice of variant depending on the:

- athlete's stage of training; and

- requirements of a sport.

Variants of these workout solutions can be used in all sports, depending on the capabilities and needs of the athletes.

*Table 1. Examples of the number of takeoffs in a workout dedicated to developing jumping ability*

| Workout variant | Training stage, athlete's level, and workout selection | | | | | | | |
|---|---|---|---|---|---|---|---|---|
| | Youth | Number of takeoffs | General stage | Number of takeoffs | Directed stage | Number of takeoffs | Sport-specific stage | Number of takeoffs |
| | Very small load | | Small load | | Medium load | | Great load | |
| 1 | 10 x 10-jump, no prerun | 100 | 6 x 15-jump, no prerun; 8 x 10-jump, no prerun; 10 x 3-jump, no prerun | 200 | 8 x 15-jump, no prerun; 10 x 10-jump, no prerun; 5 x 10-jump, with prerun; 10 x 3-jump, no prerun | 300 | 10 x 15-jump, no prerun; 8 x 10-jump, no prerun; 8 x 10-jump, with prerun; 6 x 10-jump, with prerun; 10 x 3-jump, no prerun | 400 |
| 2 | 9 x 10-jump, no prerun | 90 | 6 x 15-jump, no prerun; 6 x 10-jump, no prerun; 10 x 3-jump, no prerun | 180 | 8 x 15-jump, no prerun; 8 x 10-jump, no prerun; 5 x 10-jump, with prerun; 10 x 3-jump, no prerun | 280 | 10 x 15-jump, no prerun; 8 x 10-jump, no prerun; 6 x 10-jump, with prerun; 6 x 10-jump, with prerun; 10 x 3-jump, no prerun | 380 |

*(Table continued on the next page)*

| Workout variant | Training stage, athlete's level, and workout selection | | | | | | | |
|---|---|---|---|---|---|---|---|---|
| | Youth — Very small load | Number of takeoffs | General stage — Small load | Number of takeoffs | Directed stage — Medium load | Number of takeoffs | Sport-specific stage — Great load | Number of takeoffs |
| 3 | 3 x 10-jump, no prerun; 2 x 10-jump, with prerun; 2 x 5-jump, with prerun; 7 x 3-jump, no prerun | 81 | 6 x 15-jump, no prerun; 3 x 10-jump, with prerun; 5 x 5-jump, with prerun; 5 x 3-jump, no prerun | 160 | 6 x 15-jump, no prerun; 5 x 10-jump, no prerun; 5 x 10-jump, with prerun; 5 x 5-jump, no prerun; 5 x 5-jump, with prerun; 7 x 3-jump, no prerun | 261 | 7 x 15-jump, no prerun; 8 x 10-jump, no prerun; 8 x 10-jump, with prerun; 8 x 5-jump, no prerun; 7 x 5-jump, with prerun; 7 x 3-jump, no prerun | 361 |
| 4 | 3 x 10-jump, no prerun; 2 x 10-jump, with prerun; 2 x 5-jump, with prerun; 3 x 3-jump, no prerun | 69 | 5 x 10-jump, no prerun; 4 x 10-jump, with prerun; 6 x 5-jump, with prerun; 7 x 3-jump, no prerun | 141 | 10 x 10-jump, no prerun; 8 x 10-jump, with prerun; 8 x 5-jump, with prerun; 7 x 3-jump, no prerun | 241 | 10 x 10-jump, no prerun; 10 x 10-jump, with prerun; 8 x 10-jump, with prerun; 8 x 5-jump, with prerun; 7 x 3-jump, no prerun | 341 |
| 5 | 3 x 10-jump, no prerun; 4 x 5-jump, with prerun; 3 x 3-jump, no prerun | 59 | 4 x 10-jump, no prerun; 4 x 10-jump, with prerun; 4 x 5-jump, with prerun; 7 x 3-jump, no prerun | 121 | 6 x 10-jump, no prerun; 6 x 10-jump, with prerun; 4 x 10-jump, with prerun; 8 x 5-jump, with prerun; 7 x 3-jump, no prerun | 221 | 10 x 10-jump, no prerun; 8 x 10-jump, no prerun; 8 x 10-jump, with prerun; 8 x 5-jump, with prerun; 7 x 3-jump, no prerun | 321 |

## Sport-specific Explosive Strength for Jumping Ability

The concept of strength-jumping training must include in its program developing the type of strength that occurs in a given sport. Biomechanical research and the rich experience of coaches point to the particular importance of explosive strength in contemporary training. Its importance is greatest in those sports that have high requirements for jumping ability with a shortened amortization phase. (*Amortization* here means the gradual extinguishing of jumps, absorbing the load elastically, for example.)

Jumps occurring in various sports exhibit the same pattern: the eccentric action of the muscles of the lower limbs, when the athlete's foot contacts the ground, followed by the amortization phase, and finally the phase of concentric muscle action when muscles by their contraction permit making a transition to the takeoff phase (figure 6).

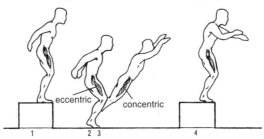

*Figure 6. Eccentric and concentric phases of jumping*

Plyometric exercises (depth jumps, for example) effectively develop strength-jumping ability for the second phase of the jump. In other words, these are exercises developing explosive strength in movements of extremely brief duration that use the immediately preceding muscle stretch (accumulating the additional energy of the reflexive contraction). During strength-jumping training, this type of exercise, using one's own body resistance, should play a significant role in contemporary training (Starzynski 1990). It must be remembered that these exercises put great stress on the joints of lower limbs. While applying them, care should be taken regarding both the way of performing them and the number of repetitions. In one workout it is safe to perform 30-50 depth jumps from different heights followed by an immediate takeoff. These exercises can be done singly or assembled into sets and are performed with different distances between takeoff spots. This difference between takeoff and landing might be up to 150 cm (5') without a prerun and approximately 200 cm (6'6") with a prerun of 3-5 steps. Choosing the height of the boxes an athlete jumps off of and the distance between these boxes is decided not only by an athlete's mass but also by his or her height. These parameters (height and distance between boxes) would be completely different for two athletes, for example, one 200 cm (6'6") tall and the other 170 cm (5'6"). Both the amount and intensity of plyometric exercises should be set individually, depending on the athlete's level of experience.

Various plyometric exercises are applied taking into consideration the needs of a given sport as well as the type of athlete (strength predisposed, speed predisposed). In practice, appropriate exercises are selected from three groups that match typical training needs. These groups of exercises are assembled according to the different needs for explosive strength.

1) Depth jumps for developing general explosive strength (figure 7)

2) Depth jumps for developing strength in eccentric actions—amortizing strength (figure 8)

3) Depth jumps for developing strength in concentric actions—takeoff after shortened amortizing phase (figure 9)

*Figure 7. Even boxes: jump down, takeoff, jump up*

*Figure 8. From higher to lower box: jump down, takeoff, jump up*

*Figure 9. From lower to higher box: jump down, takeoff, jump up*

Practical experience shows that depth jumps can be used not only for developing explosive strength but also for individual improvement in function of those weaker but essential muscle groups that often require extra work to obtain greater jumping ability.

## Sport-specific Explosive Strength for Arm Movements

In many sports it is necessary to develop—as with the example of jumping ability—explosive strength in the upper limbs, combined, of course with the technique of a given sport (Zglinicki 1993). To these sports belong nearly all events of gymnastics and acrobatics. Such explosive movements of the arms are also in rowing and kayaking. There are sports where both a high level of jumping ability of the legs and the dynamic "shock" action of the arms are needed—for example, boxing, badminton, judo, team ball games (except soccer), track-and-field throws, pole vault, tennis (lawn and table), wrestling, and martial arts.

Movements of the arms, depending on the sport, are very varied, as the following list suggests.

- Bouncing of balls (mostly volleyball)—figure 10

- Gymnastic evolutions on apparatus—figure 11

- Catching balls (basketball, team handball)—figure 12

- Passing—throwing balls (basketball, team handball)—figure 13

- Track-and-field throws—figure 14

- Goalkeeper's actions—figure 15

- Rowing—figure 16

- Breaking falls with hands (team handball, volleyball)—figure 17

- Pushing off in pole vault—figure 18

*Figure 10. Bouncing of balls—overhand and bump pass*

*Figure 11. Gymnastic evolutions on apparatus*

*Figure 12. Catching balls*

*Figure 13. Passing—throwing balls*

*Figure 14. Track-and-field throws*

*Figure 15. Goalkeeper's actions*

*Figure 16. Rowing*

*Figure 17. Breaking falls with hands*

*Figure 18. Pushing off in pole vault*

Developing the explosive strength of arm muscles should take advantage of the accumulation of additional energy resulting from the reflexive contraction of the athlete's muscles after a stretch. The effectiveness of action is decided not only by the amount of muscular tension involved in it but by the speed of muscle contraction—and thus the acceleration of movement directed toward a ball or a track-and-field implement.

Exercises with a barbell rolled on an incline (even up to 45°) are exceptionally effective in developing the explosive strength of the athlete's arms . The choice of the exercises is to be made taking into account the needs of the technique of a given sport (figures 19-24). Spotting by a partner is necessary with these exercises.

*Figure 19. Sit-up*

*Figure 20. Seated row*

*Figure 21. Press lying prone*

*Figure 22. Pulldown lying supine*

*Figure 23. Arm curl (roll the barbell up the incline)*

*Figure 24. Press (one hand at a time) lying prone*

# 3

# Exercises for Prevention of Injuries to Ankle, Knee, and Arm Joints

In contemporary training both coaches and scientists concentrate their attention on optimizing the psychophysical preparation of an athlete. Physiologists, using ever more precise apparatus and computer analysis, control the intensity of work and the state of the athletes' condition. In spite of all that, injuries often eliminate from the most serious competitions even the best-prepared athletes, contenders for world or olympic championship. One of the causes still seems to be perfunctory treatment of the process of biological recovery techniques, which include massage, hydrotherapy, thermo therapy, UV light, ultrasound, change of environment, and the use of biologically active substances. Another cause is lack of attention to prevention. Because of growing training loads, an increase of the intensity of training work, and especially of the increase in the numbers of competitions, active and purposeful prevention of overstress and injuries must be an inseparable element of contemporary training. Coaches and athletes limit themselves in practice to treatment of injuries. This pattern must change to one in which prevention occupies equal time.

In the majority of sports, injuries are caused by insufficient preparation of the most stressed muscle groups and ligaments, also by a lack of timely applied preventive exercises. This pertains in particular to the lower limbs, most often the ankle and knee joints. Occurrence of injuries can be prevented by appropriate exercises (upon consultation with rehabilitation specialists). Of great importance here are strength exercises with external resistance for the prevention of strains and sprains. Adequate muscle strength as well as high elasticity and durability of ligaments eliminate the possibility of an accidental injury (Starzynski 1987, Starzynski 1990). In every sport it is necessary to determine which muscle groups and which ligaments are most often injured and so require strengthening.

If knee and ankle joints are particularly vulnerable (for example, in jumping exercises), it is important for prevention to perform movements in all possible directions for a given joint. For example, for ankle joints not only flexion and extension are essential, but also adduction, abduction and circular movements. The exercises should be selected so as to ensure contraction of appropriate muscles through the full range of motion in the involved joints. This is ensured by exercises in the form of low hops on apparatus with variously angled surfaces (figure 25), as one way.

*Figure 25. Apparatus for performing exercises preventing injuries to ankle and knee joint*

Such apparatus allows performing a great variety of exercises. The athlete exercises during each workout, after the warm-up, observing the proper degree of difficulty for his or her status.

*Low degree of difficulty.* Youth and beginners should perform hops or jumps without additional weight (figure 26), which takes into account their unfinished skeletal development, the high vulnerability of their joint cartilage, and a low ability to withstand external loads.

*Figure 26. Exercises without additional weights on apparatus in the shapes of sections of a cylinder*

*Moderate degree of difficulty.* Hops with weights on the waist (figure 27) are applied with advanced athletes of both sexes. Loading of the joints of lower limbs is markedly greater than without weights. The center of body mass remains low, which is essential for keeping one's balance and for making coordination of movements easier.

*Figure 27. Exercises with weights on the waist on apparatus in the shapes of sections of a cylinder*

*High degree of difficulty.* Hops with a barbell weighing 30-50% of an athlete's weight (coach decides the exact weight of the barbell) are for highly advanced athletes (figure 28). Using the barbell not only increases loading of lower limbs but also raises the calculated center of combined mass of body and barbell, interfering with keeping the balance, and thus changing the distribution of forces acting on ankle and knee joints.

*Figure 28. Exercises with weights on the shoulders on apparatus in the shapes of sections of a cylinder*

The exercises that follow also develop strength of the legs, general fitness, movement coordination, and one's sense of balance. While applying them trainers and athletes must remember to prepare the mobility of ankle and knee joints through purposeful warm-up.

- Circular movements of feet by rotating ankle joints in both directions, while sitting on the floor and while lying, with knees bent and straight—for example, 20 movements alternately to the outside and to the inside while sitting with knees bent, and then while lying face up with knees straight

- Circular "twisting" movements of the trunk, while standing, with considerable leaning

Initially it is best to use apparatus shaped like a section of a cylinder—doing exercises on both the convex and concave surfaces as depicted in figures 26-28. These exercises do not require great caution and control. This is the first group of exercises.

**Examples of exercises of the first group,** with weights and without—hops on apparatus in the shapes of sections of a cylinder

- Hops sideways from left side to right side, feet together

- Hops in one spot, legs slightly astride

- Hops with quarter turn, half turn, full turn, feet together

- Hops with quarter turn, half turn, full turn, legs slightly astride

- Hops with quarter turns to the left and to the right, from left side to right side, feet together, in continuous motion

Next, the athlete progresses to exercises on apparatus of an angular shape, with two slanted surfaces contacting each other (figures 29-31). The difficulty of ankle and foot joints' work is greater here. Attention should be paid to changing the spots where feet land, either in the "valley" or on the "top of the roof." This is the second group of exercises.

*Figure 29. Hops without additional weights on apparatus of angular shape*

*Figure 30. Hops with additional weights on the waist on apparatus of angular shape*

*Figure 31. Hops with weights on the shoulders on apparatus of angular shape*

**Examples of exercises of the second group,** with weights and without—hops on apparatus of angular shape

- Hops in one spot, legs slightly astride

- Hops sideways from left side to right side, legs slightly astride

- Hops with quarter turn, legs slightly astride

- Hops in one spot, from feet together to slightly astride

The surface of the apparatus must provide secure footing—the best is a rubber mat. This permits sure and stable landings, and it is essential in exercises strengthening ligaments and joint capsules in which athlete's feet are stable but the rest of his or her body leans in any direction with additional weight. In such positions intensive effort is performed by the calf muscles that stabilize the ankle joint. In this situation these muscles work as if in "reverse" because usually they move the foot in relation to the lower leg but here the foot is stable while the lower leg moves. All this considerably increases the range and the efficiency of movements in the ankle joints, and also the fitness of lower limbs.

Also strengthened are passive elements in both ankle and knee joints. They become less susceptible to overloads, which are unavoidable in various jumps, runs, gymnastic landings, parachuting, ski jumps, team ball games, and the like.

Exercises of ankle and knee joints while standing and sitting with and without use of an inclined plane also have a preventive character (figures 32, 33), with the further plus of introducing variety to a workout. They are done after warm-up, before or during the main part of the workout. This is the third group of exercises.

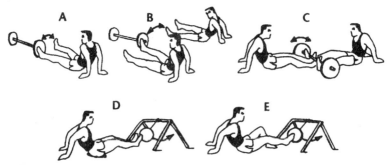

*Figure 32. Exercises of ankle and knee joint with barbell and medicine ball, while sitting*

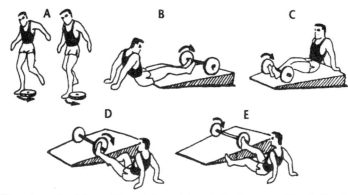

*Figure 33. Exercises of ankle and knee joint with weight plates and barbell, while standing and sitting with use of inclined planes*

**Examples of exercises of the third group**—exercises of the ankle and knee joints

- Sitting with support of the arms, pushing a barbell with feet to the inside (adduction) and to the outside (abduction) (figure 32 A)

- Sitting with support of the arms, pushing a barbell with feet to the inside (adduction) and to the outside (abduction) with partner (figure 32 B)

- Sitting with support of the arms, pulling (by dorsiflexing the feet) a barbell away from partner, pushing the barbell toward the partner (figure 32 C)

- Sitting with support of the arms, with both feet, bouncing a medicine ball suspended below a hurdle, so the feet move through the full range of motion in ankle joints (figure 32 D)

- Sitting with support of the arms, with one foot bouncing a medicine ball suspended below a hurdle so the foot moves through the full range of motion in ankle joint (figure 32 E)

- Standing on one leg, slightly bent at the knee, pushing a weight plate to the inside (adduction) and to the outside (abduction), alternating the legs (figure 33 A)

- Sitting with support of the arms, pushing the barbell up an incline so the ankle joints move through their full range of motion (figure 33 B);

- Sitting with support of the arms, pulling (by dorsiflexing the feet) the barbell up an incline, so the ankle joints move through their full range of motion (figure 33 C)

- Sitting with support of the arms, pushing to the inside (adduction) up an incline, alternating the legs (figure 33 D)

- Sitting with support of the arms, pushing to the outside (abduction) up an incline, alternating the legs (figure 33 E)

In many sports similar care to that given to the legs and feet should be given to the arms and hands. Preventing injuries of upper limbs with special exercises is an outright necessity to avoid injuries of the shoulder, elbow, or wrist. Here is a special group of exercises (figure 34), the fourth group of exercises.

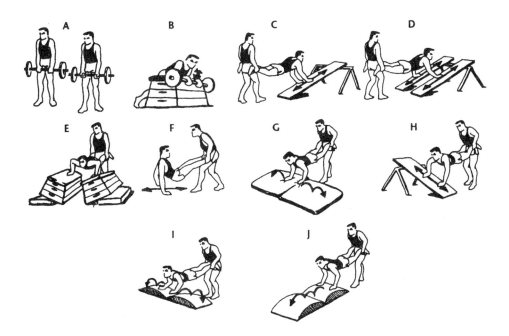

*Figure 34. Preventive exercises for arms: walking on hands, bouncing off of hands on various pieces of apparatus, set up at various angles, with and without additional weights*

**Examples of exercises of the fourth group**—exercises for the upper limbs

- Standing and holding the barbell with arms hanging down, pulling the barbell up a little and switching one's grip from overhand to underhand (figure 34 A); similar switching of grips can be done while hanging from a bar

- Standing between two gymnastic boxes or leaning on one box, arms straight and resting on top of the boxes, hands hanging over the edges of the boxes and holding a barbell in overhand grip, bending and straightening the wrists, the same with underhand grip (figure 34 B)

- Walking up and down an incline on hands, partner holding the legs (figure 34 C)

- Climbing and descending two separate inclines on hands, partner holding the legs (figure 34 D)

- Walking on hands over two gymnastic boxes that lean against each other, partner holding the legs (figure 34 E)

- Walking on hands forward and backward while sitting face up, partner holding the legs (figure 34 F)

- Walking on hands from side to side, on gymnastic pads, partner holding the legs (figure 34 G)

- Walking on hands from side to side, on an incline, with partner holding the legs (figure 34 H)

- Bouncing on hands from side to side, on apparatus in the shape of two sections of a cylinder, partner holding the legs (figure 34 I)

- Bouncing on hands forward and backward, on apparatus in the shape of two sections of a cylinder, partner holding the legs (figure 34 J)

The exercises for prevention of injuries are simple. The ones for ankles and knees have the added virtue of contributing to the development of jumping ability. The same factors that improve the function or strength of the joints—the reaction forces effects of jumping or hopping on various surfaces, with various positioning of the center of body mass—will simultaneously develop explosive strength. The increased mobility will be appropriate to the demands of the sport, which vary, of course (figure 35).

To sum it up, the proposed exercises affect improvement of the functioning of ankle joints, knees, and wrists through:

- increasing mobility in the upper and lower joints of the ankle (figures 35 and 36);

- strengthening joint capsules and ligaments;

- improved active and passive stability;

- increased mobility in joints;

- considerable increase in resilience and the durability of tissues surrounding the joint;

- elimination of even traces of spasms that limit mobility; and

- protection from accidental injuries.

*Figure 35. Difference of range of motion in the ankle joint of a gymnast (A) and a track-and-field jumper (B)*

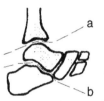

*Figure 36. Upper ankle joint (a) and lower ankle joint (b)*

# 4

# Atlas of Exercises for Jumping Ability and Explosive Strength

Before beginning to use the atlas of exercises it is advisable to read the first three chapters, pages 1-51. This will enable the reader to:

- get to know properties of the proposed groups of exercises;

- learn reasons for choosing particular exercises;

- get to know and understand the methodology of the exercises; and

- learn about the selection of preventive exercises.

The atlas contains groups of exercises most effective for developing jumping ability and explosive strength in the majority of sports. The exercises presented here are based on extensive coaching experience. Particular groups of exercises are subordinated to the needs for jumping ability in various sports, and are tied to the specifics of the technique and requirements of a sports contest. The manner of using and choosing the exercises is up to the coaches, who should use the whole gamut of presented exercises, taking into account the need to:

- vary training means;

- enrich workouts with new, unknown exercises; and

- individualize training loads with consideration for an athlete's capabilities and the requirements of the sport.

The majority of exercises will take place in sets, sometimes with, sometimes without additional weights such as sandbags, medicine balls, weighted belts and vests, and barbells.

The foundation for developing jumping ability is basic strength preparation of the lower limbs. Contemporary training ought to focus on optimizing eccentric and concentric strength as well as explosive strength. This will lead to the highest level of jumping ability.

For 16- and 17-year-olds, jumping exercises are mainly for developing strength, especially of their lower limbs, and also for developing coordination and speed. The exercise groups in this atlas are useful in the training of an athlete at all stages.

All exercises are associated with definite magnitudes of muscular tensions, shown here (figures 37-39) expressed as percentages of maximum tensions, in three basic exercises. It does not pay to overload the body!

*Figure 37. Tension (in % of maximum) of various muscles during a squat with submaximal weight (Fidelus and Kocjasz 1975). Submaximal weight is the weight that can be lifted 2-3 times without considerable mobilization of will, between approximately 90 and 93.5% of 1RM (repetition maximum).*

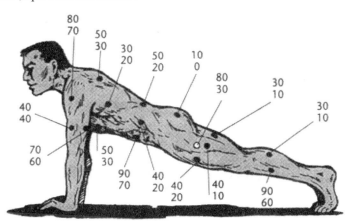

*Figure 38. Magnitude of tension of muscles (in % of maximum) during throw of the legs from a squat supported by arms to a push-up position. Upper numbers, fast movement; lower numbers, slow movement (Fidelus and Kocjasz 1975)*

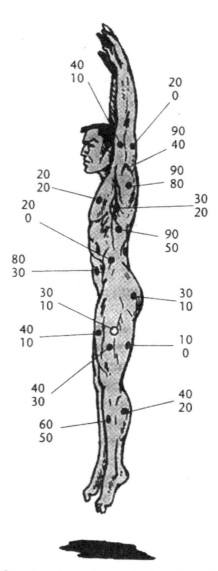

*Figure 39. Magnitude of tension of muscles (in % of maximum) during jump up from a squat supported by arms. Upper numbers, fast movement; lower numbers, slow movement (Fidelus and Kocjasz 1975)*

# Exercises for Individual Sports

Throughout the following atlas of exercises, the letters $L$ and $R$ are used to denote takeoff foot. $L$ means takeoff from left foot; $R$ means takeoff from right foot; $L/R$ means takeoff from both feet.

| Badminton | Gymnastic acrobatics | Gymnastics | Kayaking | T&F sprints, middle distance | Long jump, Triple jump | High jump | Pole vault | Discus, Hammer, Shot | Javelin | Speed skating | Cross-country skiing | Downhill skiing | Ski jumping | Swimming | Luge | Parachuting | Lawn tennis | Table tennis | Rowing | Exercise | Description of exercise |
|---|---|---|---|---|---|---|---|---|---|---|---|---|---|---|---|---|---|---|---|---|---|
| | | | | | | | | | | | | | | | | | | | | **Multijumps** | |
| • | | | | | • | • | • | • | • | • | • | • | • | | • | | • | • | | | 10-jump, left-right, no prerun |
| • | | | | | • | • | • | • | • | • | • | • | • | | • | | • | • | | | 10-jump, left-right, with prerun |
| • | | | | | • | • | | • | | | | | | | | | | | | | 10-jump on one leg, no prerun |
| • | | | | | • | • | | • | | | | | | | | | | | | | 10-jump on one leg, with prerun |
| • | | | | | • | • | • | | | | | | | | | | | | | | 10-jump in double rhythm: left, left-right, right, no prerun |
| • | | | | | • | • | • | | | | | | | | | | | | | | 10-jump in double rhythm: left, left-right, right, with prerun |

| Badminton | Gymnastic acrobatics | Gymnastics | Kayaking | T&F sprints, middle distance | Long jump, Triple jump | High jump | Pole vault | Discus, Hammer, Shot | Javelin | Speed skating | Cross-country skiing | Downhill skiing | Ski jumping | Swimming | Luge | Parachuting | Lawn tennis | Table tennis | Rowing | Type of exercise | Exercise | Description of exercise |
|---|---|---|---|---|---|---|---|---|---|---|---|---|---|---|---|---|---|---|---|---|---|---|
|  | • | • |  |  |  |  |  | • |  |  |  | • | • |  | • | • |  |  |  | Multijumps |  | 10-jump on both legs, no prerun |
|  | • | • |  |  |  |  |  | • |  |  |  | • | • | • | • | • |  |  |  |  |  | 10-jump over obstacles, on both legs, short prerun |
|  |  |  |  |  | • | • | • | • |  |  |  | • |  |  |  |  |  |  |  |  |  | 10-jump over obstacles, on one leg, short prerun |
|  |  |  |  |  |  |  |  |  |  | • | • |  |  |  |  |  |  |  |  |  |  | 10-jump "zigzag" over a ditch (outdoor) |
|  |  |  |  |  |  |  |  |  |  |  |  |  |  |  | • |  |  |  |  |  |  | 10-jump on a curve, left-right, always go to the left, no prerun |
|  |  |  |  |  |  |  |  |  |  |  |  |  |  |  | • |  |  |  |  |  |  | 10-jump on a curve, left-right, always go to the left, 5-step prerun |

| Badminton | Gymnastic acrobatics | Gymnastics | Kayaking | T&F sprints, middle distance | Long jump, Triple jump | High jump | Pole vault | Discus, Hammer, Shot | Javelin | Speed skating | Cross-country skiing | Downhill skiing | Ski jumping | Swimming | Luge | Parachuting | Lawn tennis | Table tennis | Rowing | Type of exercise | Exercise | Description of exercise |
|---|---|---|---|---|---|---|---|---|---|---|---|---|---|---|---|---|---|---|---|---|---|---|
| • | | | | | • | • | • | | | | | | | | | | | | | Multijumps | | 5-jump, left-right, no prerun |
| • | | | | | • | • | • | | | | | | | | | | | | | | | 5-jump, left-right, with prerun |
| • | | | | | • | • | • | | | | | | | | | | | | | | | 5-jump on one leg, no prerun |
| • | | | | | • | • | • | | | | | | | | | | | | | | | 5-jump on one leg, with prerun |
| | • | • | | | | | | • | • | | | | • | | | | | | | | | 5-jump, on both legs, no prerun |
| | | | | | • | • | | • | | | | | | | | | | | | | | 3-jump, no prerun |

| Badminton | Gymnastic acrobatics | Gymnastics | Kayaking | T&F sprints, middle distance | Long jump, Triple jump | High jump | Pole vault | Discus, Hammer, Shot | Javelin | Speed skating | Cross-country skiing | Downhill skiing | Ski jumping | Swimming | Luge | Parachuting | Lawn tennis | Table tennis | Rowing | Type of exercise | Exercise | Description of exercise |
|---|---|---|---|---|---|---|---|---|---|---|---|---|---|---|---|---|---|---|---|---|---|---|
| • | • | • |  |  |  | • |  | • |  |  |  |  | • | • |  | • | • |  |  | Reach jumps |  | reach jump from a squat in spot, to full extension of hips |
| • | • | • |  |  |  | • |  | • |  |  |  |  | • | • |  | • | • |  |  |  |  | reach jump from a squat in spot, to full extension of hips, with weighted belt |
| • |  |  |  |  |  | • |  |  |  |  |  | • | • |  |  |  |  |  |  |  |  | jump with two-leg takeoff, no prerun, and reach the ball with hand |
| • |  |  |  |  |  | • | • |  |  |  |  | • | • |  |  |  |  |  |  |  |  | jump with two-leg takeoff, with a short prerun, and reach the ball with hand |
|  |  |  |  |  |  | • | • |  |  |  |  |  | • |  |  |  |  |  |  |  |  | jump with two-leg takeoff, no prerun, and reach the ball with forehead |
|  |  |  |  |  | • | • |  |  |  |  |  |  | • |  |  |  |  |  |  |  |  | jump with two-leg takeoff, with a prerun, and reach the ball with forehead |

| Badminton | Gymnastic acrobatics | Gymnastics | Kayaking | T&F sprints, middle distance | Long jump, Triple jump | High jump | Pole vault | Discus, Hammer, Shot | Javelin | Speed skating | Cross-country skiing | Downhill skiing | Ski jumping | Swimming | Luge | Parachuting | Lawn tennis | Table tennis | Rowing | Type of exercise | Exercise | Description of exercise |
|---|---|---|---|---|---|---|---|---|---|---|---|---|---|---|---|---|---|---|---|---|---|---|
| • | | | | | • | • | | | | | | | | | | | | | | Reach jumps | | jump with a short prerun and reach the ball with a knee |
| | | | | | | • | | | | | | | | | | | | | | | | jump with a short prerun and reach the ball with a foot (leg slightly bent at knee) |
| | | | | | • | • | | | | | | | | | | | | | | | | with both feet jump up on a box 30-60 cm high (1-2 feet), immediately, with one foot jump off the box and land in sand pit or on a pad |
| • | | | | | • | • | | | | | | | | | | • | | | | | | jump off one foot resting on the box |
| • | | | | | • | • | | | | | | | | | | • | | | | | | after a short prerun, jump up on a box, land on the other foot and jump off it |

| Badminton | Gymnastic acrobatics | Gymnastics | Kayaking | T&F sprints, middle distance | Long jump, Triple jump | High jump | Pole vault | Discus, Hammer, Shot | Javelin | Speed skating | Cross-country skiing | Downhill skiing | Ski jumping | Swimming | Luge | Parachuting | Lawn tennis | Table tennis | Rowing | Type of exercise | Exercise | Description of exercise |
|---|---|---|---|---|---|---|---|---|---|---|---|---|---|---|---|---|---|---|---|---|---|---|
| • | | | | | • | • | | | | | | | | | | | • | | | Reach jumps | | jump on and off the box, take off by the side of the box with the same leg |
| • | | | | | • | • | | | | | | | | | | | • | | | | | jump on and off boxes (set up so you can take off with the same foot) |
| • | | | | | • | • | | | | | | | | | | | • | | | | | jump up from a one-leg takeoff by the side of the increasingly higher boxes |
| | | | | | • | • | | | | | | | | | | | | | | | | jump up from a one-leg takeoff by the side of a gymnastic bench or beam slanted up |
| | | | | | • | • | • | | | | | | | | | | | | | Takeoff exercises | | jump up on boxes from left leg to right leg |

63

| Badminton | Gymnastic acrobatics | Gymnastics | Kayaking | T&F sprints, middle distance | Long jump, Triple jump | High jump | Pole vault | Discus, Hammer, Shot | Javelin | Speed skating | Cross-country skiing | Downhill skiing | Ski jumping | Swimming | Luge | Parachuting | Lawn tennis | Table tennis | Rowing | Type of exercise | Exercise | Description of exercise |
|---|---|---|---|---|---|---|---|---|---|---|---|---|---|---|---|---|---|---|---|---|---|---|
|  |  |  |  |  | • | • | • |  |  | • |  |  |  |  |  |  |  |  |  | Takeoff exercises | | jump up on boxes from left leg to right leg, with weighted belt |
|  |  |  |  |  | • | • | • |  |  | • |  |  |  |  |  |  |  |  |  |  | | jump up on increasingly higher boxes from left leg to right leg |
|  |  |  |  |  | • | • | • |  |  | • |  |  |  |  |  |  |  |  |  |  | | jump up on gymnastic benches or beams slanted up, from left leg to right leg |
|  |  |  |  |  | • | • | • |  |  | • | • | • |  |  |  |  |  |  |  |  | | jump from one tilted box onto the other |
|  |  |  |  |  |  | • | • |  |  | • | • | • |  |  |  |  |  |  |  |  | | jump from one tilted box onto the other, with weight (sandbag) on shoulders |
| • |  |  |  |  | • | • |  |  |  |  |  |  |  |  |  |  |  | • |  |  | | jump (with an intermediate landing on the bench or beam) from one side of the bench or beam to the other |

| Badminton | Gymnastic acrobatics | Gymnastics | Kayaking | T&F sprints, middle distance | Long jump, Triple jump | High jump | Pole vault | Discus, Hammer, Shot | Javelin | Speed skating | Cross-country skiing | Downhill skiing | Ski jumping | Swimming | Luge | Parachuting | Lawn tennis | Table tennis | Rowing | Type of exercise | Exercise | Description of exercise |
|---|---|---|---|---|---|---|---|---|---|---|---|---|---|---|---|---|---|---|---|---|---|---|
| • | | | | | • | • | | | | | | | | | | | • | | | Takeoff exercises | | jump from one side of the bench or beam to the other (with an intermediate landing on top), barbell on shoulders |
| | | | | | • | • | | | | | | | | | | | | | | Heel-to-toe push-off | | from a lunge with one foot on top of the box, swing up the other leg's knee and rise on toes |
| | | | | | • | • | | | | | | | | | | | | | | | | from a lunge with one foot on top of the box, swing up the other leg's knee and rise on toes, weight on shoulders |
| | | | | | • | • | | | | | | | | | | | | | | | | from a lunge with one foot on top of the slanted box, swing up the other leg's knee and rise on toes |

| Badminton | Gymnastic acrobatics | Gymnastics | Kayaking | T&F sprints, middle distance | Long jump, Triple jump | High jump | Pole vault | Discus, Hammer, Shot | Javelin | Speed skating | Cross-country skiing | Downhill skiing | Ski jumping | Swimming | Luge | Parachuting | Lawn tennis | Table tennis | Rowing | Type of exercise | Exercise | Description of exercise |
|---|---|---|---|---|---|---|---|---|---|---|---|---|---|---|---|---|---|---|---|---|---|---|
|  |  |  |  |  | • | • |  |  |  |  |  |  |  |  |  |  |  |  |  | Heel-to-toe push-off | | from a lunge with one foot on top of the slanted box, swing up the other leg's knee and rise on toes, weight on shoulders |
|  |  |  |  |  | • | • |  |  |  |  |  |  |  |  |  |  |  |  |  |  | | sit in front of the box and push it away with both legs (in imitation of takeoff—from heel to toe) |
|  |  |  |  |  | • | • |  |  |  |  |  |  |  |  |  |  |  |  |  |  | | sit in front of the box and push it off with one leg (in imitation of takeoff—from heel to toe) |
| • | • | • |  | • | • | • | • | • | • | • |  | • | • | • |  |  |  | • | • | Hopping | | jump rope |

| Description of exercise | Type of exercise | Rowing | Table tennis | Lawn tennis | Parachuting | Luge | Swimming | Ski jumping | Downhill skiing | Cross-country skiing | Speed skating | Javelin | Discus, Hammer, Shot | Pole vault | High jump | Long jump, Triple jump | T&F sprints, middle distance | Kayaking | Gymnastics | Gymnastic acrobatics | Badminton |
|---|---|---|---|---|---|---|---|---|---|---|---|---|---|---|---|---|---|---|---|---|---|
| hopping side to side on a convex surface | Hopping | • | • |  | • | • | • | • | • | • | • | • | • | • | • | • | • | • | • | • | • |
| hopping side to side on a convex surface, with weighted belt |  | • | • |  | • | • | • | • | • | • | • | • | • | • | • | • | • | • | • | • | • |
| hopping side to side on a convex surface, with weight on shoulders |  | • | • |  | • | • | • | • | • | • | • | • | • | • | • | • | • | • | • | • | • |
| hopping side to side on a concave surface |  | • | • |  | • | • | • | • | • | • | • | • | • | • | • | • | • | • | • | • | • |
| hopping side to side on a concave surface, with weighted belt |  | • | • |  | • | • | • | • | • | • | • | • | • | • | • | • | • | • | • | • | • |
| hopping side to side on a concave surface, with weight on shoulders |  |  | • |  |  |  |  | • | • | • | • | • | • | • | • | • | • | • | • | • | • |

| Badminton | Gymnastic acrobatics | Gymnastics | Kayaking | T&F sprints, middle distance | Long jump, Triple jump | High jump | Pole vault | Discus, Hammer, Shot | Javelin | Speed skating | Cross-country skiing | Downhill skiing | Ski jumping | Swimming | Luge | Parachuting | Lawn tennis | Table tennis | Rowing | Type of exercise | Exercise | Description of exercise |
|---|---|---|---|---|---|---|---|---|---|---|---|---|---|---|---|---|---|---|---|---|---|---|
| | | | | | | | | | | | | | | | | | | | | Depth jumps | | |
| • | • | • | | • | • | • | • | • | • | • | • | • | • | | | | • | • | • | | | jump down-jump up, feet together, between two boxes |
| • | | | | | | | • | • | • | | | | | | | | • | • | | | | jump down-jump up, on one foot, between two boxes |
| • | • | • | | • | • | • | • | • | • | • | • | • | | • | | | • | • | • | | | jump down from a lower box, jump up on a higher box, feet together |
| • | | | | | • | • | • | | | | | | | | | | • | • | • | | | jump down from a lower box, jump up on a higher box, on one foot |
| • | • | • | | • | • | • | • | • | • | • | • | • | | • | | | • | • | • | | | jump down from a higher box, jump up on a lower box, feet together |
| • | | | | | | • | • | • | | | | | | | | | • | • | | | | jump down from a higher box, jump up on a lower box, on one foot |

| Badminton | Gymnastic acrobatics | Gymnastics | Kayaking | T&F sprints, middle distance | Long jump; Triple jump | High jump | Pole vault | Discus, Hammer, Shot | Javelin | Speed skating | Cross-country skiing | Downhill skiing | Ski jumping | Swimming | Luge | Parachuting | Lawn tennis | Table tennis | Rowing | Type of exercise | Description of exercise |
|---|---|---|---|---|---|---|---|---|---|---|---|---|---|---|---|---|---|---|---|---|---|
| • | • | • | | • | • | • | • | • | • | • | • | • | • | • | | | • | • | • | Depth jumps | jump down from one box, jump up on the other, then jump off, all takeoffs with both feet |
| • | | | | | • | • | • | | | | | | • | • | | | | | | | jump down from one box, jump up on the other, then jump off, all takeoffs with one foot |
| • | • | • | | • | • | • | • | • | • | • | • | • | • | • | | | • | • | • | | jump down from lower box, jump up on the higher, then jump off, all takeoffs with both feet |
| • | • | | | | • | • | • | | | | | | • | • | | | | | | | jump down from lower box, jump up on the higher, then jump off, all takeoffs with one foot |
| • | • | • | | • | • | • | • | • | • | • | • | • | • | | • | | | | • | | jump down from higher box, jump up on the lower, then jump off, all takeoffs with both feet |

| Type of exercise | Exercise | Description of exercise | Badminton | Gymnastic acrobatics | Gymnastics | Kayaking | T&F sprints, middle distance | Long jump, Triple jump | High jump | Pole vault | Discus, Hammer, Shot | Javelin | Speed skating | Cross-country skiing | Downhill skiing | Ski jumping | Swimming | Luge | Parachuting | Lawn tennis | Table tennis | Rowing |
|---|---|---|---|---|---|---|---|---|---|---|---|---|---|---|---|---|---|---|---|---|---|---|
| Depth jumps | | jump down from higher box, jump up on the lower, then jump off, all takeoffs with one foot | • | • | | | | • | • | • | | | | | | | | | | • | • | |
| | | after a depth jump take off with both feet to reach a suspended ball | | | | | | • | • | | | | | | | | | | | | | |
| | | jump down, upon landing immediately do long jump off both legs | • | | • | • | | • | • | • | • | • | • | • | • | • | • | • | • | • | • | • |
| | | jump down, upon landing immediately do long jump off one leg | • | • | | | | • | • | • | | | | | | | | | • | • | • | |
| | | jump off the box and land on one and then on the other foot (triple jump from a box) | | | | | | • | • | | | | | | | | | | | | | |

70

| Badminton | Gymnastic acrobatics | Gymnastics | Kayaking | T&F sprints, middle distance | Long jump, Triple jump | High jump | Pole vault | Discus, Hammer, Shot | Javelin | Speed skating | Cross-country skiing | Downhill skiing | Ski jumping | Swimming | Luge | Parachuting | Lawn tennis | Table tennis | Rowing | Type of exercise | Exercise | Description of exercise |
|---|---|---|---|---|---|---|---|---|---|---|---|---|---|---|---|---|---|---|---|---|---|---|
| | | | | | • | • | | | | | | | | | | | | | | Depth jumps | | triple jump, without prerun, first takeoff with one leg resting on the box 30-60 cm (1-2 feet) |
| | | | | | • | | | | | | | | | | | | | | | | | triple jump, first takeoff with both legs from the box 40-100 cm (16-40") , make third jump from both feet, over an obstacle 50-80 cm (20-32") |
| | | | | | • | | | | | | | | | | | | | | | | | triple jump with 3-5 steps of prerun, first takeoff from a box 20-30 cm (8-12") |
| | | | | | • | | | | | | | | | | | | | | | | | triple jump with 3-5 steps of prerun, second takeoff from a box 20-30 cm/8-12" |
| | | | | | • | | | | | | | | | | | | | | | | | triple jump with 3-5 steps of prerun, third takeoff from a box 30-60 cm (1-2 feet) |

| Description of exercise | Badminton | Gymnastic acrobatics | Gymnastics | Kayaking | T&F sprints, middle distance | Long jump, Triple jump | High jump | Pole vault | Discus, Hammer, Shot | Javelin | Speed skating | Cross-country skiing | Downhill skiing | Ski jumping | Swimming | Luge | Parachuting | Lawn tennis | Table tennis | Rowing | Exercise |
|---|---|---|---|---|---|---|---|---|---|---|---|---|---|---|---|---|---|---|---|---|---|
| sit and roll the barbell inward with your foot | • | • | • | | • | • | • | • | • | • | • | • | • | • | • | • | • | • | • | • | Ankle and knee |
| sit and roll the barbell inward with your foot, up an incline | • | • | • | | • | • | • | • | • | • | • | • | • | • | • | • | • | • | • | • | |
| sit and roll the barbell outward with your foot, toward a partner | • | • | • | | • | • | • | • | • | • | • | • | • | • | • | • | • | • | • | • | |
| sit and roll the barbell outward with your foot, up an incline | • | • | • | | • | • | • | • | • | • | • | • | • | • | • | • | • | • | • | • | |
| sit and take turns with your partner at pulling the barbell toward yourself by dorsiflexion of feet | • | • | • | | • | • | • | • | • | • | • | • | • | • | • | • | • | • | • | • | |
| sit on an incline and pull the barbell toward yourself by dorsiflexion of feet | • | • | • | | • | • | • | • | • | • | • | • | • | • | • | • | | • | | • | |

| Type of exercise | Exercise | Description of exercise | Badminton | Gymnastic acrobatics | Gymnastics | Kayaking | T&F sprints, middle distance | Long jump, Triple jump | High jump | Pole vault | Discus, Hammer, Shot | Javelin | Speed skating | Cross-country skiing | Downhill skiing | Ski jumping | Swimming | Luge | Parachuting | Lawn tennis | Table tennis | Rowing |
|---|---|---|---|---|---|---|---|---|---|---|---|---|---|---|---|---|---|---|---|---|---|---|
| Ankle and knee | | with your leg slightly bent at the knee, push a weight plate inward (adduction) and outward (abduction) | • | • | • | • | • | • | • | • | • | • | • | • | • | • | • | • | • | • | • | • |
| | | push the barbell to your partner, move ankle joints through full ROM | • | | | | • | • | • | • | • | • | • | | | | • | | | • | • | • |
| | | push the barbell up an incline, move ankle joints through full ROM | • | | | | | • | • | • | • | • | • | | | | • | | | • | • | • |
| | | bounce with both feet a suspended medicine ball, move ankle joints through full ROM | • | | | | • | • | • | • | • | • | • | | | | • | | | • | • | • |
| | | bounce with one foot a suspended medicine ball, move ankle joint through full ROM | • | | | | | • | • | • | • | • | • | | | | • | | | • | • | • |

73

| Badminton | Gymnastic acrobatics | Gymnastics | Kayaking | T&F sprints, middle distance | Long jump, Triple jump | High jump | Pole vault | Discus, Hammer, Shot | Javelin | Speed skating | Cross-country skiing | Downhill skiing | Ski jumping | Swimming | Luge | Parachuting | Lawn tennis | Table tennis | Rowing | Type of exercise | Exercise | Description of exercise |
|---|---|---|---|---|---|---|---|---|---|---|---|---|---|---|---|---|---|---|---|---|---|---|
| • | • | • |  |  |  |  | • | • | • |  |  |  |  | • |  |  |  |  | • | Arm exercises |  | standing barbell press |
| • | • | • |  |  |  |  | • | • | • |  |  |  |  | • |  |  |  |  | • |  |  | sitting barbell press |
| • | • | • |  |  |  |  | • | • | • |  |  |  |  | • |  |  |  |  | • |  |  | bench press |
| • | • | • |  |  |  |  | • | • | • |  | • |  |  | • |  |  |  |  | • |  |  | stand with one foot on the inclined box, rise on your toes while pressing up the barbell |
| • | • | • |  |  |  |  | • | • | • |  | • |  |  | • |  |  |  |  | • |  |  | lie prone and with both arms roll the barbell on the floor; use over- and underhand grip |

| Badminton | Gymnastic acrobatics | Gymnastics | Kayaking | T&F sprints, middle distance | Long jump, Triple jump | High jump | Pole vault | Discus, Hammer, Shot | Javelin | Speed skating | Cross-country skiing | Downhill skiing | Ski jumping | Swimming | Luge | Parachuting | Lawn tennis | Table tennis | Rowing | Type of exercise | Exercise | Description of exercise |
|---|---|---|---|---|---|---|---|---|---|---|---|---|---|---|---|---|---|---|---|---|---|---|
| | | | | | | | | | | | | | | | | | | | | | Arm exercises | |
| • | • | • | | | | | • | • | • | | • | | | • | | | | | • | | | lie prone and with both arms push the barbell so it rolls to your partner; use over- and underhand grip |
| • | • | • | | | | | • | • | • | | | | | • | | | | | • | | | lie prone and with both arms press the barbell up an incline; use both over- and underhand grip |
| | | | | | | | | • | • | | | | | | | | | | | | | lie prone and with one arm press the barbell up an incline; use both over- and underhand grip |
| • | • | • | | | | | • | • | • | | | | • | | | | | | • | | | lie prone and with both arms push away the barbell up an incline; use both over- and underhand grip |

| Badminton | Gymnastic acrobatics | Gymnastics | Kayaking | T&F sprints, middle distance | Long jump, Triple jump | High jump | Pole vault | Discus, Hammer, Shot | Javelin | Speed skating | Cross-country skiing | Downhill skiing | Ski jumping | Swimming | Luge | Parachuting | Lawn tennis | Table tennis | Rowing | Type of exercise | Exercise | Description of exercise |
|---|---|---|---|---|---|---|---|---|---|---|---|---|---|---|---|---|---|---|---|---|---|---|
|  |  |  |  |  |  | • | • | • |  |  |  |  |  |  |  |  |  |  |  | Arm exercises |  | lie prone and with one arm push away the barbell up an incline; use over- and underhand grip |
|  |  |  | • |  |  |  |  |  |  |  | • |  |  |  |  |  |  |  |  |  |  | lie prone, and alternating your arms, press the barbell up an incline; use both over- and underhand grip |
|  |  |  | • |  |  |  |  |  |  |  | • |  |  |  |  |  |  |  |  |  |  | lie prone, and alternating arms, push away the barbell up an incline; use both over- and underhand grip |
| • | • | • |  |  |  | • | • | • |  |  | • |  | • |  |  |  | • |  |  |  |  | chin-up |
|  |  |  |  |  |  |  | • | • |  |  |  |  |  |  |  |  |  |  |  |  |  | one-hand chin-up |

| Type of exercise | Exercise | Description of exercise |
|---|---|---|
| | **Arm exercises** | |
| | | hang on the bar, pull to "jump off" the bar (head above the bar) |
| | | hang on the bar, through a forward and then backward swing of legs, enter support on both arms |
| | | hang on the bar, pull up to support on both arms (one movement) |
| | | with both arms push away a suspended barbell, while standing, sitting, kneeling, lying |
| | | with one arm push away a suspended barbell, while standing, sitting, kneeling, lying |

Type of exercise (sports listed):
Badminton, Gymnastic acrobatics, Gymnastics, Gymnastics, Kayaking, T&F sprints, middle distance, Long jump, Triple jump, High jump, Pole vault, Discus, Hammer, Shot, Javelin, Speed skating, Cross-country skiing, Downhill skiing, Ski jumping, Swimming, Luge, Parachuting, Lawn tennis, Table tennis, Rowing

Markings (•) per exercise:

| Sport | Exercise 1 | Exercise 2 | Exercise 3 | Exercise 4 | Exercise 5 |
|---|---|---|---|---|---|
| Badminton | | | | • | • |
| Gymnastic acrobatics | | | | | |
| Gymnastics | • | • | • | | |
| Gymnastics | • | • | • | | |
| Kayaking | • | • | • | | |
| T&F sprints, middle distance | | | | | |
| Long jump, Triple jump | | | | | |
| High jump | | | | | |
| Pole vault | • | • | • | | |
| Discus, Hammer, Shot | • | • | • | | |
| Javelin | • | • | • | • | • |
| Speed skating | | | | | |
| Cross-country skiing | | | | | |
| Downhill skiing | | | | | |
| Ski jumping | | | | | |
| Swimming | • | • | • | | |
| Luge | | | | | |
| Parachuting | | | | | |
| Lawn tennis | • | • | • | • | • |
| Table tennis | • | • | • | | |
| Rowing | • | • | • | | |

77

| Badminton | Gymnastic acrobatics | Gymnastics | Kayaking | T&F sprints, middle distance | Long jump, Triple jump | High jump | Pole vault | Discus, Hammer, Shot | Javelin | Speed skating | Cross-country skiing | Downhill skiing | Ski jumping | Swimming | Luge | Parachuting | Lawn tennis | Table tennis | Rowing | Type of exercise | Exercise | Description of exercise |
|---|---|---|---|---|---|---|---|---|---|---|---|---|---|---|---|---|---|---|---|---|---|---|
| • | | | | | | | | • | | | | | | | | | • | | | Arm exercises | | lie supine between two inclined planes, with both arms push the barbell up |
| | • | • | | | | | | • | • | | | | | • | | | • | | | | | kneel and push the barbell with both arms underhand to your partner |
| | • | • | | | | | | • | • | | | | | • | | | • | | | | | kneel and push the barbell with both arms underhand up an incline |
| | • | • | | | | | | | | | | | | | | | | | • | | | sit and lean forward between two inclined planes, then pull the barbell up until you lie supine |
| • | • | • | • | | | | • | • | • | • | | • | • | | | | • | • | • | | | hold the bar in straight arms, quickly switch grips from overhand to underhand |

78

| Type of exercise — Arm exercises | | | | | | | | | | | | | | | | | | | | | Exercise | Description of exercise |
|---|---|---|---|---|---|---|---|---|---|---|---|---|---|---|---|---|---|---|---|---|---|---|
| Badminton | Gymnastic acrobatics | Gymnastics | Gymnastics | Kayaking | T&F sprints, middle distance | Long jump, Triple jump | High jump | Pole vault | Discus, Hammer, Shot | Javelin | Speed skating | Cross-country skiing | Downhill skiing | Ski jumping | Swimming | Luge | Parachuting | Lawn tennis | Table tennis | Rowing | | |
| • | • | • | | | | | | • | • | • | | | | | • | | | | | • | | standing arm curl |
| • | • | • | | | | | | • | • | • | | | | | • | | | | | • | | standing arm curl, back and heels touch the wall |
| • | • | • | | | | | | • | • | • | | | | | • | | | | | • | | kneeling arm curl |
| • | • | • | | | | | | • | • | • | | | | | • | | | | | • | | sitting arm curl |
| • | • | | | | | | | | • | • | | | | | • | | • | | | | | lying arm curl, elbows on the floor |
| • | • | • | | • | | | | | • | • | | | | | • | | | | | | | sit between two inclined planes, pull the barbell up (imitate rowing) with both arms |

| Badminton | Gymnastic acrobatics | Gymnastics | Kayaking | T&F sprints, middle distance | Long jump, Triple jump | High jump | Pole vault | Discus, Hammer, Shot | Javelin | Speed skating | Cross-country skiing | Downhill skiing | Ski jumping | Swimming | Luge | Parachuting | Lawn tennis | Table tennis | Rowing | Type of exercise | Exercise | Description of exercise |
|---|---|---|---|---|---|---|---|---|---|---|---|---|---|---|---|---|---|---|---|---|---|---|
|  | • | • | • |  |  |  |  | • | • |  |  |  |  | • |  |  |  |  | • | Arm exercises | | sit between two inclined planes, pull the barbell up with one arm at a time |
|  | • | • | • |  |  |  |  |  |  |  | • |  |  |  |  |  |  |  | • |  | | sit between two inclined planes, pull one side of the barbell up at a time (imitate kayaking) |
|  | • | • |  |  |  |  |  |  |  |  | • |  | • |  |  |  |  |  |  |  | | lift up the bench from the floor with a partner sitting on it, underhand grip |
|  | • | • |  |  |  |  |  |  |  |  | • |  | • |  |  |  |  |  |  |  | | lift up the bench from your hip height with a partner sitting on it, underhand grip |
|  |  |  | • |  |  |  | • |  |  |  | • |  |  |  |  |  |  |  | • |  | | rope climb using arms only |

**80**

| Description of exercise | Exercise | Type of exercise | Rowing | Table tennis | Lawn tennis | Parachuting | Luge | Swimming | Ski jumping | Downhill skiing | Cross-country skiing | Speed skating | Javelin | Discus, Hammer, Shot | Pole vault | High jump | Long jump, Triple jump | T&F sprints, middle distance | Kayaking | Gymnastics | Gymnastic acrobatics | Badminton |
|---|---|---|---|---|---|---|---|---|---|---|---|---|---|---|---|---|---|---|---|---|---|---|
| rope climb by short "jumps" using arms only | | Arm exercises | • | • |  |  |  |  |  |  | • |  |  |  |  |  |  |  | • |  |  |  |
| legs up on a support, bounce on your hands on two convex surfaces, change width of arms | |  | • | • | • |  |  |  |  |  | • |  | • | • | • |  |  |  | • | • | • |  |
| walk up and down an inclined bench with partner holding your legs | |  | • | • | • |  |  |  |  |  |  |  | • | • | • |  |  |  | • | • | • |  |
| walk up and down two parallel inclined benches with partner holding your legs | |  | • | • | • |  |  |  |  |  | • |  | • | • | • |  |  |  | • | • | • |  |

81

**6**

# Exercises for Team Games

| Basketball | Ice hockey | Field hockey | Soccer | Team handball | Rugby | Volleyball | Type of exercise | Exercise | Description of exercise |
|---|---|---|---|---|---|---|---|---|---|
| • | | | • | • | • | • | Multijumps | | 10-jump, left-right, no prerun |
| • | | | • | • | • | • | | | 10-jump, left-right, with prerun |
| • | | | • | • | • | • | | | 10-jump on one leg, no prerun |
| • | | | • | • | • | • | | | 10-jump on one leg, with prerun |
| | | | • | • | • | • | | | 10-jump on both legs, no prerun |
| • | | | • | • | • | • | | | 5-jump, left-right, no prerun |

| Basketball | Ice hockey | Field hockey | Soccer | Team handball | Rugby | Volleyball | Type of exercise | Exercise | Description of exercise |
|---|---|---|---|---|---|---|---|---|---|
| • | • | • |  | • | • |  | Multijumps | | 10-jump "zigzag" over a ditch (outdoor) |
| • | • | • |  | • | • |  |  | | 10-jump "zigzag" over a ditch (outdoor), with prerun |
| • | • | • | • | • | • | • |  | | 5-jump, on both legs, no prerun |
| • | • | • | • | • | • | • |  | | 10-jump over obstacles, on both legs, no prerun |
| • | • | • | • | • | • | • |  | | 10-jump over obstacles, on one leg (change leg with every set), no prerun |
| • | • | • | • | • | • | • |  | | 10-jump over obstacles, on both legs, or on one leg (change leg with every set), as in two preceding exercises, but with a short prerun |

| Basketball | Ice hockey | Field hockey | Soccer | Team handball | Rugby | Volleyball | Type of exercise | Exercise | Description of exercise |
|---|---|---|---|---|---|---|---|---|---|
| • | • | • | • | • | • | • | Reach jumps | | reach jump from a squat in spot, to full extension of hips |
| • | • | • | • | • | • | • | | | reach jump from a squat in spot, to full extension of hips, with weighted belt |
| • | | | | • | • | • | | | jump with two-leg takeoff, no prerun, and reach the ball with hand |
| • | | | | • | • | • | | | jump with either one- or two-leg takeoff, with a short prerun, and reach the ball with hand |
| | | | • | | | • | | | jump with two-leg takeoff, no prerun, and reach the ball with forehead |
| | | | • | | | • | | | jump with two-leg takeoff, with a prerun, and reach the ball with forehead |

| Basketball | Ice hockey | Field hockey | Soccer | Team handball | Rugby | Volleyball | Type of exercise | Exercise | Description of exercise |
|---|---|---|---|---|---|---|---|---|---|
| | | | | | | | Reach jumps | | jump with two-leg takeoff, no prerun, and reach the ball with a knee |
| | | • | • | | • | | | | jump with either one- or two-leg takeoff, prerun, and reach the ball with a knee |
| | | | • | | | | | | jump with a short prerun and reach the ball with a foot (leg slightly bent in knee), one-leg takeoff |
| | | | | • | • | • | | | jump and grab a bar, change distance from the bar 30-50-70-90-100 cm (12-20-28-36-40 inches) |
| • | | • | • | • | • | | | | make three leaps after a short prerun, and jump on the gymnastic stalls to land on one foot |
| • | | • | • | • | • | | | | make three leaps after a short prerun, and jump on the gymnastic stalls to land on both feet |

87

| Basketball | Ice hockey | Field hockey | Soccer | Team handball | Rugby | Volleyball | Type of exercise | Exercise | Description of exercise |
|---|---|---|---|---|---|---|---|---|---|
| • | • | • | • | • | • | • | Depth jumps | | jump down-jump up, feet together, between two boxes of equal height |
| • | • | • | • | • | • | • | | | jump down-jump up, on one foot, between two boxes of equal height |
| • | • | • | • | • | • | • | | | jump down from a lower box, jump up on a higher box, feet together |
| • | • | • | • | • | • | • | | | jump down from a lower box, jump up on a higher box, on one foot |
| • | • | • | • | • | • | • | | | jump down from a higher box, jump up on a lower box, feet together |
| • | • | • | • | • | • | • | | | jump down from a higher box, jump up on a lower box, on one foot |

| Basketball | Ice hockey | Field hockey | Soccer | Team handball | Rugby | Volleyball | Type of exercise | Exercise | Description of exercise |
|---|---|---|---|---|---|---|---|---|---|
| • |  | • | • | • | • | • | Depth jumps | | jump down from one box, jump up on the other, then jump off, all takeoffs with both feet, boxes of equal height |
| • |  | • | • | • | • | • | Depth jumps | | jump down from one box, jump up on the other, then jump off, all takeoffs with one foot, boxes of equal height |
| • | • | • | • | • | • | • | Takeoff exercises | | jump (with an intermediate step on top) from one to the other side of a row of boxes |
| • | • | • | • | • | • | • | Takeoff exercises | | jump (with an intermediate step on top) from one to the other side of a row of increasingly higher boxes |
| • | • | • | • | • | • | • | Takeoff exercises | | jump (with an intermediate step on top) from one to the other side of a slanted gymnastic bench or beam; at the end, hold on to the gymnastic stall and repeat jumps in place |
| • | • | • | • | • | • | • | Takeoff exercises | | jump up on boxes from left leg to right leg |

| Basketball | Ice hockey | Field hockey | Soccer | Team handball | Rugby | Volleyball | Type of exercise | Exercise | Description of exercise |
|---|---|---|---|---|---|---|---|---|---|
| • | • | • | • | • | • | • | Takeoff exercises | | jump up on boxes from left leg to right leg, with weighted belt |
| | • | | | • | | | | | jump from one tilted box onto the other |
| | • | | | • | | | | | jump from one tilted box onto the other, with weight (sandbag) on shoulders |
| • | | | • | • | • | • | | | jump over boxes (set up so you can take off with the same foot) with an intermediate step on top |
| • | | | • | • | • | • | | | jump (with an intermediate landing on the bench or beam) from one side of the bench or beam to the other |
| • | | | • | • | • | • | | | jump from one side of the bench or beam to the other (with an intermediate landing on top), barbell on shoulders |

| Basketball | Ice hockey | Field hockey | Soccer | Team handball | Rugby | Volleyball | Type of exercise | Exercise | Description of exercise |
|---|---|---|---|---|---|---|---|---|---|
| • | • | • | • | • | • | • | Hopping | | hop in place, on both feet, keep changing position of feet (in, out, both point left or right) |
| • | • | • | • | • | • | • | | | hopping side to side on a convex surface |
| • | • | • | • | • | • | | | | hopping side to side on a convex surface, with weighted belt |
| • | • | • | • | • | • | • | | | hopping side to side on a concave surface |
| • | • | • | • | • | • | • | | | hopping side to side on a concave surface, with weighted belt |
| • | • | • | • | • | | • | Ankle and knee | | bounce with both feet a suspended medicine ball, move ankle joints through full range of motion |

91

| Basketball | Ice hockey | Field hockey | Soccer | Team handball | Rugby | Volleyball | Type of exercise | Exercise | Description of exercise |
|---|---|---|---|---|---|---|---|---|---|
| | | | | | | | Ankle and knee | | bounce with one foot a suspended medicine ball, move ankle joint through full range of motion |
| • | • | • | • | • | • | • | | | hop and with your leg slightly bent at the knee, push a weight plate inward (adduction) and outward (abduction) |
| • | • | • | • | • | • | • | | | with the inside of your foot push a medicine ball to bounce it off the wall, alternate feet with every push |
| • | • | • | • | • | • | • | | | push the barbell to your partner, move ankle joints through full range of motion |
| • | • | • | • | • | • | • | | | push the barbell up an incline, move ankle joints through full range of motion |
| • | • | • | • | • | • | • | | | sit and roll the barbell outward and inward with your foot, toward a partner |

| Basketball | Ice hockey | Field hockey | Soccer | Team handball | Rugby | Volleyball | Type of exercise | Exercise | Description of exercise |
|---|---|---|---|---|---|---|---|---|---|
| | | | | | | | | | |
| • | • | • | • | • | • | • | Ankle and knee | | sit and roll the barbell inward and outward with your foot, up an incline |
| • | • | • | • | • | • | • | | | sit and take turns with your partner at pulling the barbell toward yourself by dorsiflexion of feet |
| • | • | • | • | • | • | • | | | sit on an incline and pull the barbell toward yourself by dorsiflexion of feet |
| | | • | • | • | • | | | | stand in a deep lunge and with your front shin and foot push the medicine ball so it flies to your partner |
| | | | • | • | • | | Arm exercises | | from a pushup position, hands on a medicine ball, throw the medicine ball up and forward; your feet should rise off the floor too |
| • | | | • | • | • | | | | lunge forward to throw and bounce a medicine ball off the wall, alternate legs with every throw |

| Basketball | Ice hockey | Field hockey | Soccer | Team handball | Rugby | Volleyball | Type of exercise | Exercise | Description of exercise |
|---|---|---|---|---|---|---|---|---|---|
| • | • | • | • | • | • | • | Arm exercises | | with both hands throw a medicine ball so it bounces off the floor behind you, quickly squat and twist to catch it on the first bounce, twist to alternate sides with every throw |
| • | | | • | • | • | | | | bench press |
| • | | | • | • | • | | | | stand with one foot on the inclined box, rise on your toes while pressing up the barbell |
| • | | | • | • | • | | | | lie prone and with both arms roll the barbell on the floor; use over- and underhand grip |
| • | | | • | • | • | | | | lie prone and with both arms push the barbell so it rolls to your partner; use over- and underhand grip |
| • | | | • | • | • | | | | lie prone and with both arms press the barbell up an incline; use both over- and underhand grip |

| Basketball | Ice hockey | Field hockey | Soccer | Team handball | Rugby | Volleyball | Type of exercise | Exercise | Description of exercise |
|---|---|---|---|---|---|---|---|---|---|
| | | | | | | | Arm exercises | | |
| • | | | | • | • | • | | | lie prone and with one arm press the barbell up an incline; use both over- and underhand grip |
| • | | | | • | • | • | | | lie prone and with both arms push away the barbell up an incline; use both over- and underhand grip |
| • | | | | • | • | • | | | lie prone and with one arm push away the barbell up an incline; use both over- and underhand grip |
| • | | | | | • | • | | | hang on the bar, pull to "jump off" the bar (head above the bar) |
| • | | | | • | • | • | | | hang on the bar, through a forward and then backward swing of legs, enter support on both arms |
| • | | | | | • | • | | | hang on the bar, pull up to support on both arms (one movement) |

Exercises for Team Games

| Basketball | Ice hockey | Field hockey | Soccer | Team handball | Rugby | Volleyball | Type of exercise | Exercise | Description of exercise |
|---|---|---|---|---|---|---|---|---|---|
| • | | | | • | | | Arm exercises | | from kneeling, jump and grab a bar or gymnastic rings |
| • | | | | • | | | | | from kneeling, with a weight belt on, jump and grab a bar or gymnastic rings |
| • | | | | • | • | • | | | with both arms push away a suspended barbell, while standing, sitting, kneeling, lying |
| • | | | | • | • | • | | | with one arm push away a suspended barbell, while standing, sitting, kneeling, lying |
| • | | | | • | • | • | | | lie supine between two incline planes, with both arms push the barbell up |
| • | | | | • | • | • | | | kneel and push the barbell with both arms underhand to your partner |

| Basketball | Ice hockey | Field hockey | Soccer | Team handball | Rugby | Volleyball | Type of exercise | Exercise | Description of exercise |
|---|---|---|---|---|---|---|---|---|---|
| | | | | | | | | | |
| • | | | • | | • | • | Arm exercises | | kneel and push the barbell with both arms underhand up an incline |
| • | • | • | • | • | • | • | | | hold the bar in straight arms, quickly switch grips from overhand to underhand |
| • | | | • | | • | • | | | standing arm curl |
| • | | | • | | • | • | | | standing arm curl, back and heels touch the wall |
| • | | | • | | • | • | Arm exercises (bounce) | | in a pushup position, bounce off the floor with hands |
| • | | | • | | • | • | | | in a pushup position, bounce on both hands around a circle; feet stay in the center of the circle |

**97**

| Basketball | Ice hockey | Field hockey | Soccer | Team handball | Rugby | Volleyball | Type of exercise | Exercise | Description of exercise |
|---|---|---|---|---|---|---|---|---|---|
| • |  |  |  | • | • | • | Arm exercises (bounce) | | in a pushup position, legs up on a support, with hands bounce off the floor |
| • | • | • |  | • |  | • |  | | legs up on a support, bounce on your hands on two convex surfaces, change width of arms |
| • | • | • |  | • |  | • |  | | walk up and down an inclined bench with partner holding your legs |
| • | • | • |  | • |  | • |  | | walk up and down two parallel inclined benches with partner holding your legs |

# 7

# Exercises for Combat Sports

Martial artists who do jumping techniques, such as flying kicks, should add to the following exercises the reach jumps shown on page 61 (especially the two exercises at the bottom of the page), page 62, page 86, and the three top exercises on page 87.

| Boxing | Kickboxing | Judo | Fencing | Wrestling | Type of exercise | Exercise | Description of exercise |
|---|---|---|---|---|---|---|---|
| • | • | • | • | • | Multijumps | | 10-jump, left-right, no prerun |
| • | • | • | • | • | | | 10-jump, left-right, with prerun |
| • | • | • | • | • | | | 10-jump on one leg, no prerun |
| • | • | • | • | • | | | 10-jump on one leg, with prerun |
| • | • | • | • | • | | | 10-jump on both legs, no prerun |
| • | • | • | • | • | | | 10-jump over obstacles, on both legs, no prerun |

| Boxing | Kickboxing | Judo | Fencing | Wrestling | Type of exercise | Exercise | Description of exercise |
|---|---|---|---|---|---|---|---|
| | | | | | Multijumps | | 10-jump over obstacles, on one leg, no prerun |
| • | • | • | • | • | | | |
| • | • | • | | • | Takeoff exercises | | jump (with an intermediate step on top) from one to the other side of a row of boxes |
| • | • | • | • | • | | | jump (with an intermediate step on top) from one to the other side of a row of increasingly higher boxes |
| • | • | • | • | • | | | jump (with an intermediate step on top) from one to the other side of a slanted gymnastic bench or beam; at the end, hold on to the gymnastic stall and repeat jumps in place |
| • | • | • | | • | | | jump up on boxes from left leg to right leg |
| • | • | • | • | • | | | jump up on gymnastic benches or beams slanted up, from left leg to right leg |

**101**

| Boxing | Kickboxing | Judo | Fencing | Wrestling | Type of exercise | Exercise | Description of exercise |
|---|---|---|---|---|---|---|---|
| | | | | | **Takeoff exercises** | | jump (with an intermediate landing on the bench or beam) from one side of the bench or beam to the other |
| • | • | • | | • | | | |
| | | | | | | | jump from one side of the bench or beam to the other (with an intermediate landing on top), barbell on shoulders |
| • | • | • | | • | | | |
| | | | | | **Depth jumps** | | jump down-jump up, feet together, between two boxes |
| • | • | • | • | • | | | |
| | | | | | | | jump down-jump up, on one foot, between two boxes |
| • | • | • | • | • | | | |
| | | | | | | | jump down from a higher box, jump up on a lower box, feet together |
| • | • | • | • | • | | | |
| | | | | | | | jump down from a higher box, jump up on a lower box, on one foot |
| • | • | • | • | • | | | |

102

| Boxing | Kickboxing | Judo | Fencing | Wrestling | Type of exercise | Exercise | Description of exercise |
|---|---|---|---|---|---|---|---|
| • | • | | | | Hopping | | jump rope, bounce on both feet |
| • | • | | | | | | jump rope, bounce on alternate feet |
| • | • | • | • | • | | | hop in place, with weighted belt, on both feet, keep changing position of feet (in, out, both point left or right) |
| • | • | • | • | • | | | hopping side to side on a convex surface |
| • | • | • | • | • | | | hopping side to side on a concave surface |
| • | • | • | • | • | | | hopping side to side on a convex surface, with weighted belt |

**103**

| Boxing | Kickboxing | Judo | Fencing | Wrestling | Type of exercise | Exercise | Description of exercise |
|--------|-----------|------|---------|-----------|------------------|----------|-------------------------|
| • | • | • | • | • | Hopping | | hopping side to side on a concave surface, with weighted belt |
| • | • |  |  |  | Ankle and knee | | bounce with both feet a suspended medicine ball, move ankle joints through full range of motion |
| • | • |  |  |  |  | | bounce with one foot a suspended medicine ball, move ankle joint through full range of motion |
| • | • | • | • | • |  | | hop and with your leg slightly bent at the knee, push a weight plate inward (adduction) and outward (abduction) |
| • | • | • | • | • |  | | sit and take turns with your partner at pulling the barbell toward yourself by dorsiflexion of feet |
| • | • | • | • | • |  | | push the barbell to your partner, move ankle joints through full range of motion |

| Boxing | Kickboxing | Judo | Fencing | Wrestling | Type of exercise | Exercise | Description of exercise |
|---|---|---|---|---|---|---|---|
| | | | | | Ankle and knee | | push the barbell up an incline, move ankle joints through full range of motion |
| • | • | • | • | • | | | |
| • | • | • | • | • | | | sit on an incline and pull the barbell toward yourself by dorsiflexion of feet |
| | • | | | | | | stand in a deep lunge and with your front shin and foot push the medicine ball so it flies to your partner |
| | • | | | | | | sit leaning back on your arms, push with tops of both your feet to throw a medicine ball to a partner |
| | • | | | | | | sit leaning back on your arms, push with top of one foot to throw a medicine ball to a partner |
| | • | | | | Arm exercises | | from a pushup position, hands on a medicine ball, throw the medicine ball up and forward; your feet should rise off the floor too |

**105**

| Boxing | Kickboxing | Judo | Fencing | Wrestling | Type of exercise | Exercise | Description of exercise |
|---|---|---|---|---|---|---|---|
| • | • | • | • | • | Arm exercises | | lunge forward to throw and bounce a medicine ball off the wall, alternate legs with every throw |
| • | • | • |  | • | | | bounce off the wall with both hands, gradually increase distance from the wall |
| • | • | • |  | • | | | bounce off the wall with one hand, gradually increase distance from the wall |
| • | • | • | • | • | | | in a pushup position, bounce off the floor with hands |
| • | • | • |  | • | | | in a pushup position, bounce on both arms around a circle; feet stay in the center of the circle |
| • |  | • |  | • | | | in a pushup position, legs up on a support, with hands bounce off the floor |

| Boxing | Kickboxing | Judo | Fencing | Wrestling | Type of exercise | Exercise | Description of exercise |
|---|---|---|---|---|---|---|---|
| • | • | • | • | • | Arm exercises | | legs up on a support, bounce on your hands on two convex surfaces, change width of arms |
| • | • | • | • | • | | | walk up and down an inclined bench with partner holding your legs |
| • | • | • | • | • | | | walk up and down two parallel inclined benches with partner holding your legs |
| • | • | • | | • | | | hang on the bar, pull to "jump off" the bar (head above the bar) |
| • | • | • | | • | | | hang on the bar, through a forward and then backward swing of legs, enter support on both arms |
| • | • | • | | • | | | hang on the bar, pull up to support on both arms (one movement) |

| Boxing | Kickboxing | Judo | Fencing | Wrestling | Type of exercise | Exercise | Description of exercise |
|--------|-----------|------|---------|-----------|------------------|----------|-------------------------|
| | | • | | • | Arm exercises | | kneeling between two inclined planes, pull up the barbell with both arms |
| • | • | • | • | • | | | sit and lean forward between two inclined planes, then pull the barbell up until you lie supine |
| • | • | • | | • | | | lie prone and with both arms push the barbell so it rolls to your partner; use over- and underhand grip |
| • | • | • | • | • | | | hold the bar in straight arms, quickly switch grips from overhand to underhand |
| • | • | • | | • | | | lie prone and with both arms press the barbell up an incline; use both over- and underhand grip |
| • | • | • | | • | | | lie prone and with both arms push away the barbell up an incline; use both over- and underhand grip |

| Boxing | Kickboxing | Judo | Fencing | Wrestling | Type of exercise | Exercise | Description of exercise |
|---|---|---|---|---|---|---|---|
| | | | | | Arm exercises | | lie prone, and alternating your arms, twist the barbell on the floor |
| • | • | • | | • | | | lie prone, and alternating your arms, press the barbell up an incline; use both over- and underhand grip |
| • | • | • | | • | | | |

**109**

# 8

# Supplementary Strength Exercises

| Exercise | Description of exercise |
|---|---|
| | squat with acceleration, rise up on toes, barbell on shoulders |
| | half-squat with acceleration, rise up on toes, barbell on shoulders |
| | half-squat with jump, barbell on shoulder |
| | leg press, with both legs |
| | leg press, with one leg |
| | low hops with barbell on shoulders |

| Exercise | Description of exercise |
|---|---|
| | hop side to side on a convex surface, barbell on shoulders |
| | hop side to side on a concave surface, barbell on shoulders |
| | rise up on toes, toes on a four-inch step, barbell on shoulders |
| | from kneeling switch to a squat, barbell on shoulders |
| | from kneeling, pull (hang clean) the barbell to chest, and simultaneously switch to a squat |
| | from kneeling, pull (snatch) the barbell overhead, and simultaneously switch to a squat |

| Exercise | Description of exercise |
|---|---|
| | march forward in lunge position with barbell on shoulders |
| | repeated lunge forward from standing upright (alternate legs), barbell on shoulders |
| | from standing upright repeated lunge forward (alternate legs) with simultaneous pull (hang clean) of the barbell to chest |
| | from standing upright repeated lunge forward (alternate legs) with simultaneous pull (snatch) of the barbell overhead |
| | from standing upright repeated lunge forward (alternate legs) with simultaneous overhead press of the barbell from chest |
| | barbell on shoulders, in a power rack, rise on toes of one leg simultaneously swinging up the knee of the other leg |

| Exercise | Description of exercise |
|---|---|
| | barbell on shoulders, in a power rack, rise on toes of one leg simultaneously swinging up the knee of the other leg, additional weight on the swinging knee |
| | hang by both arms from a bar or gymnastic stall, swing right knee up to the left so it rests on top of the box 20-40 cm (8-16 inches), 2-4 kg (4.5-9 lb.) additional weight on the knee, exercise both legs in sets of 6-8 repetitions |
| | hold barbell in straight arms, lean trunk forward, and then straighten to pull it up |

# Bibliography

Balsevich, V. K., Zaporozhanov, V. A. 1987. *Fizicheskaya aktivnost cheloveka.* Kiev: Zdrovya.

Fidelus, K., Kocjasz, J. 1975. *Atlas cwiczen fizycznych.* Warszawa: PFS.

Grosser, M., Starischka, S., Zimmermann, E. 1989. *Konditionstraining.* Münich: BLV Sportwissen.

Hadzelek, K., ed. 1986. *Mala Encyclopedia Sportu.* Vol. 2. Warszawa: Sport i Turystyka.

Martin, D., Carl, K., Lehnertz, K. 1991. *Handbuch Trainingslehre.* Schorndorf: Verlag Hofman.

Mroczynski, Z., Starzynski, T. 1994. *Trening skoku w dal i trójskoku.* Gdansk: AWF.

Sozanski, H. 1987. *Skok wzwyz.* Warszawa: MAW.

Sozanski, H., Sledziewski D. (ed). 1989. *Technologia dokumentowania i opracowywania danych o obciazeniach treningowych.* Warszawa: RCMSzKFiS.

Starzynski, T. 1987. *Le Triple Saut.* Paris: Vigot.

Starzynski, T. 1990. "Cwiczenia plyometryczne dla trójskoku." *Sport Wyczynowy* no. 5-6.

Tidow, G. 1990. "Aspects of strength training in athletics." *New Studies in Athletics* no. 1.

Verkhoshansky YU. V. 1988. *Osnovy spetsial'noy fizicheskoy podgotovki sportsmenov.* Moskva: Fizkultura i Sport.

Zglinicki, J. 1993. "Trenerska koncepcja pomiaru obciazen treningowych w pilce recznej." *Trening* no. 2.

# Index

**V**

Velocity of movement, 6
  maximal, 6
  speed and, 7
Volleyball, 40
  ankle and knee exercises, 91–93
  arm exercises, 93–98
  depth jumps, 88–89
  hopping, 91
  multijumps, 84–85
  reach jumps, 86–87
  takeoff exercises, 89–90

**W**

Warm-up, 46
  exercises in, 4
Weightlifting, 3
Workout
  coordination exercises in, 23
  depth jumps during, 19
  exercises in, 33
  speed exercises in, 8
Wrestling
  ankle and knee exercises, 104–105
  arm exercises, 106–109
  depth jumps, 102
  explosive strength and, 40
  hopping, 103–104
  multijumps, 100–101
  takeoff exercises, 101–102

**Y**

Yearly training cycle
  coordination exercises in, 23
  jumping ability in, 32
  rotation of training means in, 33–34
  speed training in, 8
  strength training in, 17